*Ancient Pagan Symbols*

ISIS
(Museo Nazionale, Naples.)

# Ancient Pagan Symbols

Elisabeth Goldsmith

*with*
*Forty-eight Illustrations*

Ibis Press
*An Imprint of Nicolas-Hays, Inc.*
Berwick, Maine

Published in 2003
by Ibis Press
An Imprint of Nicolas-Hays, Inc.
P. O. Box 1126
Berwick, ME 03901-1126
www.nicolashays.com

**Distributed by Red Wheel/Weiser LLC**
Box 612
York Beach, ME 03901-0612
www.redwheelweiser.com

**Library of Congress Cataloging-in-Publication Data**
Goldsmith, Elisabeth, b. 1860.
    Ancient pagan symbols / Elisabeth Goldsmith.
        p. cm.
    Originally published: New York: G.P. Putnam's Sons, 1929.
    Includes index.
    ISBN 0-89254-072-9 (pbk. : alk. paper)
    1. Symbolism. 2. Mythology. 3. Art and mythology. I. Title.
BL600.G6 2003
291.3'7--dc21                    2003045277

Cover design by Alden Cole

Printed in the United States of America
BJ

09 08 07 06 05 04 03
9 8 7 6 5 4 3 2 1

# CONTENTS

## ILLUSTRATIONS

# Illustrations

# PREFACE

In offering this handbook as a companion volume to *Sacred Symbols in Art*, which deals exclusively with the symbolism found in Christian art, it is hoped that a brief interpretation of some of the meanings underlying the symbolism found in temples, on ancient ruins and monuments, and constantly reappearing as art motifs on rugs, tapestries, porcelains and bronzes, may quicken the interest and add to the enjoyment of students and travellers to Egypt and the Far East.

It is well understood by artists and architects that the designs that have been repeated down the centuries, and of which we never grow tired, may almost without exception be traced back to the Life motif. The number also that have sprung from the lotus, the swastika and the Assyrian Tree of Life will easily be recalled. These forms of art expression are seemingly like the octave in music, capable of infinite expansion.

Believing that a clearer idea will be obtained, I have, as in the companion volume on Christian symbolism, treated the subjects generically. Thus, the symbols of the Elements which play such an important part in ancient religions are given first:

then the Lotus, which is also a beginning symbol,
the Tree of Life, the Dual Principles or the Active
and Passive forces that create life, the Cross, the
Serpent, the Chinese Trigrams, the Four Supernatural
Creatures of the Chinese, Animal Symbolism in
Chinese Art, the Sun, the Moon, the Wheel symbol,
the Swastika, Ancient Gods and Goddesses, Twice-
born Gods, Sacred Birds, Sacred Animals, the Trisula,
the Triangle, also a number of General Symbols that
do not come under any special heading, but have a
more or less important bearing on ancient art.

Much of the material used here has been derived
from a previous and larger volume on *Life Symbols*.

ELISABETH GOLDSMITH.

NEW YORK,
   March, 1929.

# INTRODUCTION

I⊤ requires only a slight knowledge of symbolism to see that many of the most cherished symbols found in Christian art did not originate with the Christians, but were used in other and more ancient religions as emblems of highest import, expressing the symbolic idea of life.

If in the Christian religion the meaning is lifted to Everlasting Life which finds its revelation in Christ the Spirit of Love; if the early Christians, affronted by a corrupt paganism, seemed sternly bent on refusing all place to woman [1] and equally bent on disregarding the body of man as something unutterably vile, [2] these same symbols as used by the pagans who saw Life Everlasting in the continuity of life, gave overwhelming importance to Man and Woman, or the positive and negative forces that create life.

These apparently insignificant lines that form the upright, the cross, the circle, the triangle, have been interpreted by pathologists and psychologists, have

[1] "At the time of Christ, sexuality was so easily obtainable that it resulted in great depreciation of woman." Jung's *Psychology of the Unconscious*, p. 255.

[2] See Chapter on Triangle, *Life Symbols*.

furnished material for the artist and mystic, but it is
as a study of Man and Woman that they touch the
profoundest depths. It is doubtful whether they
could have such vital and undying interest for us
were they not the symbols of ourselves—of sex, if you
like, but of more than sex. They typify with an
implacable accuracy that astounds, the whole nature,
the inalterable nature of the two forces that create life.

If one would know man and the unknowable woman
—understand the impulses that move her apparently
so mysteriously—one has only to study their strange
and conflicting relationship as revealed in these ancient
symbols that come down to us from prehistoric days.

Once having done this, the most thrilling romance
ever written pales before the absorbing interest that
is excited by the heartbreaking differences, the inter-
mittent struggles for supremacy, for understanding,
for reconciliation, for peace that is the history of this
diametrically opposed yet passionately loving pair.

Primitive man, as far back as we can safely go,
seems to have had the same desire to know the secret
of life—still an impenetrable mystery—the same
dream of an Unknown and Almighty God, high above
all other gods, whose majesty and power rules the
universe (the thought of a *primum mobile* is often
dim, obscure, but appears to be ever lurking back in
his consciousness), the same recognition of duality,

the same urge for unity of the antagonistic forces that create life—(a unity that results in the triad or the mystical three in one.)

Then as now he was confronted by the mystery of the Life force—the *libido*, the *élan vital* which he felt in himself and surging all about him. He found it in the ebbing tides of the sea, in the flowing rivers, in the teeming earth, in the rushing, sighing winds, in the trees that stretched toward heaven, and his entire religion reflects the most intense reverence for Life, not only of how life was come by, but of its continuity through the processes of generation and re-generation. Thus he made images and drawings of the male and female organs of generation![1] It may have been self-worship—the recognition of himself as the highest known creator of life that made him exalt the phallus as a symbol of omnipotent power. One may add here that the idea promulgated by writers of a past generation, such as Inman and Knight, that this use of the organs of procreation was made with obscene intent and showed the bestiality of primitive man, is not so generally accepted by more recent in-vestigators.[2]

[1] The *lingam* and *yoni* still found extensively as religious symbols in the Far East.

[2] "To ward off ills caused by demons, especially the demons of disease, the ancient Japanese sought the protection of a particular group of gods, the Sahe no Kami, or 'preventive deities'. . . . The deities were represented by phalli, often of

The very fact that so much symbolism can be traced back to the phallus—pillars, church spires, the maypole, etc., would seem to indicate that so long as his civilisation was sound it was used reverently, not as a symbol of sex alone, but as a supreme and august symbol of creative power.

Whether knowledge came to primitive man by divine revelation or was obtained empirically, we are obliged to admit that he must have been a thinker. His records display, not a mastery, not yet has man achieved that, but an extraordinary comprehension of Life. He thought less in grooves, gave freer play to his imagination, perhaps, than now; knew life from living it and not from books, never dreaming how many books would be written about him saying how little or how much he knew of life.

---

gigantic size, which were set up along highways and especially at cross roads to bar the passage against malignant beings who sought to pass. . . . The phallic form of the end post of a balustrade or a bridge has a similar meaning; it keeps evil influence from passing. The apotropaic virtue of this symbol, a virtue it has in many other countries, notably among the ancient Greeks, is due to the association of virility with manly strength, power to overcome invisible foes as well as visible, and to protect those in need of help. Standing as they did on the roadside and at cross roads, these gods . . . had nothing to do, so far as the evidence shows, with fertility or the reproductive functions; no peculiar rites were observed in their worship, and however objectionable to the taste of a more refined age, the cult was in no sense immoral or conducive to immorality." Moore's *History of Religions*, Vol. I, pp. 107 and 108.

In his passion for life he levied everywhere through-out the entire realm of nature for symbols of fecundity, of productivity. He created a vast cosmogony. He peopled the stars that jewel the heavens. He understood the value of polarity; that fire and water, positive and negative, man and woman, spirit and matter or form were necessary complements to each other.

Knowing this, it was, possibly in an endeavour to be fair that the two opposite forces, Man and Woman, should divide up the universe between them, yet the symbolism remains perfect. The earth, air, water, moon and some of the stars belong to Woman. The sun, the primal, energising power belongs to Man. Mountains, caverns, caves, everything that is sinuous, curved, or a receptacle, are symbols of Woman. Whatever is sharp, pointed, direct, is a symbol of Man.

There were Father gods and Mother goddesses, and conviction seems to have swayed more than once as to which was the more important factor in reproducing life.[1] Sometimes the ancient placed the Supreme God in the masculine sun, the source of all light and warmth, and again in the feminine and beneficent moon whom he regarded as the source of all moisture. Much of his symbolism, however, reflects the conjunction of the divine pair, the union

[1] See *Life Symbols*, Chapter on "Father Gods and Mother Goddesses."

of sun and moon, active and passive, fire and water, man and woman, light and darkness as necessary agents of fertility.

Possibly to allay controversy, he invented bi-sexual gods, and in seeking for examples to illustrate the idea, he worshipped the serpent, lotus, scarabæus and palm tree as androgynous symbols of life. The bearded Aphrodite may have been a despairing effort to compose into one by a visible sign these opposing forces that have been such jealous and disturbing creators of life. If Man could have swallowed Woman or have been swallowed by her, no doubt living would have been smooth and harmonious, although possibly less interesting for both. And there would have been no symbolism to record the intense, dramatic interplay, ever-recurrent, ever new; nothing to show the passionate desire to curb and harness together these two principles, masculine and feminine, that are so widely divergent, yet so absolutely essential to each other. They could and did ride over and make nonentities of each other. But to dispense with each other so long as the continuity of life was the goal . . . .

Impossible!

In his sane moments Man knew that balance was the thing, but how often he deviates, goes mad, forgets—becomes so feverishly active that he worships only himself, tires of himself, and goes off in search of new gods, of strange and bizarre symbols that no longer represent creative power—forgets the sublime and awe-inspiring need of equilibrium—forgets that the passive has a part to play—forgets Woman!

Primitive man also deified certain animals whom he associated with the sun and moon and various nature gods and goddesses as symbols of reproductive power. He is, however, strangely silent about the ape. (*Perhaps he knew.*) Why, once having had a nice warm, furry skin, he should have discarded it in the interests of evolution and forever after spend fabulous sums on woollens and silks and furs to cover his shivering body—why he should have hampered himself thus has, indeed, never been satisfactorily explained. For that matter, however, his whole history during the evolutionary process offers lively gaps to the imagination.

In the Egyptian religion the baboon or dog-faced ape is given to the moon-god Thoth and is depicted sitting on the scales of justice in the judgment scene, and there are the familiar "three mystic monkeys" whose images are found along the roadsides in Japan. But, the recognition, the reverence due to an ancestor —of that, so far as we are able to learn, ancient religious art reveals not a trace.

Primitive man not only ignores the ape as father but excludes *all* fathers.

And here we have a most illuminating example of Man's ability to keep out of a situation in which he takes no pride. The Greeks, whose philosophy was a sunny one, conceded that it was better never to have been born. In bringing such a messy world into being (a doubtful blessing), although still in that infantile stage where we delight to picture him, Man was astute enough to dodge any and all responsibility and give the entire credit to Woman.

His desire to evade responsibility for anything that seems of questionable good crops out again and again in Man's history, proving possibly Jung's theory of the "collective unconscious," and that the long, long trail back to the beginning man finds him much the same.

The earliest creation myths picture "Chaotic darkness brooding over a waste of waters." Nothing exists save the Chaos Demon. She is the Great Mother self-created and self-sustaining, a Virgin goddess with a fatherless son. As the mother of the gods she is the origin of good. She is also the spirit of malevolence and would destroy the life she has created. It is she who would hold back summer and it is her son, the spirit of Life and Love, who defeats the goddess Mother and brings warmth and growth to the icebound earth.

From these earliest germs of thought on how we came into being, thus Woman comes down to us as Chaos, good insomuch as she is the mother of the gods, but evil in that she would destroy that which she has created.

The world once launched without his help, suddenly out of nowhere, giving no account of himself, quite unheralded and without explanation Man appears, and assumes the rein as the primary principle of Life. And it is here, probably, that symbolism begins. From now on, except in those periods of temporary eclipse, Man is symbolised by order; Woman is disorder. (Out of Chaos comes order. That is the divine process.) Man is everything fine, noble, high. Woman the passive or negative principle, is everything low, mean, ignoble. Man is concentrated—intense— his symbol is the sun. Woman is diffuse, expansive —she is the earth, moon, air, water, sky. Yet the connection between sun and earth is an obviously necessary one. As the Earth Mother, Woman looks up. He looks down. Thus they pass down the ages and all goes well. She is really very humble minded. She likes to look up. In no way can Man wound her so much as when he makes it no longer possible for her to look up. All goes well with the Earth Mother— (she asks so very little), till one day she discovers that he is not looking down but looking around.

We may not judge him too harshly. Man has many goddesses. Is not Woman air, water, sky, moon, as well as the stable earth?

Woman has but one god—the sun that stands

supreme above all else, is everything that is fine and high, the concentrated essence of life. Here again we must see how perfect, despairingly perfect for the peace of mind of the Earth Woman—is the symbolism. The sun's rays touch everywhere—nothing could live without the sun. It is order, strength, majesty. It is also the Great Lover, the Great Fecundator . . .

The Earth Woman is indifferent to this. Her hold on Man is something so assured, so vital that it astounds and bewilders her when he forgets. His sunny, smiling way of letting his rays dart everywhere has not disturbed her. She is only conscious of the warmth of his embrace and of their purpose together as creators of life.

But when he forsakes her, abandons her . . . One may assume, indeed, one could hardly assume otherwise, that even while fulfilling his duty to Mother Earth, Man, the incorrigible amorist has many amours, must have them, in truth, if he is to discover the undiscoverable Woman in all her variety. While pursuing his established course, he encounters sky women, star women, he circles the earth with the moon-goddess trailing after him, his rays embrace Aphrodite as she springs from the foam of the sea. These love affairs are brief, passionate, evanescent. He remains majestically silent about them. It is scarcely an exaggeration to say that Man has the arms of Kwan-yin—"she of a thousand arms" when it comes to keeping his numerous love affairs up his sleeve. An adept at secrecy (and as these occur in the natural order of things) he manages to conceal them, and at the same time preserve an attitude of calm efficiency, as he goes about his daily affairs, that completely deceives the Earth Woman.

It is not so difficult. Most of his other goddesses are as casual as he—light o' loves, loving many, appealing to the imagination, to the roving, seeking nature of Man. Their rôle is a generic one embracing many aspects. That of the Earth goddess is specific, narrowed to the one relationship. To her, Man who is her god, who represents the sun, is more than all else a good husbandman. The word explains itself.

In his long and adventurous career, Man could and did substitute one god for another without apparently any appreciable suffering or any great sense of loss, rather with the exhilaration of one who had discovered something new.

Not so when he deserts the Earth goddess. He seems to lose all sense of proportion when he ceases to have contact with Mother Earth. She represents stability, puts the solid earth under his feet. Paradoxically, he can only reach the heights by keeping his feet on the ground. With her he suffers torments. Of all his goddesses she is the most exacting. She disciplines him even while looking up to him. She is inexorable in her demands on him, for she, too, has a passion for productivity. She makes him earn his bread by the sweat of his brow, gives him only enough reward for his labour to keep body and mind strong and healthy, and the world goes on peacefully. The fecund Earth is happily absorbed in her great purpose. The sun, whose rays shine upon all, does not forget to caress and warm her, even as he seeks out others who are less dependent and less responsive.

All goes well with the Earth Woman till Man forgets her, forgets caution and instead of shining like his great prototype, the sun, lavishly and impartially upon all, concentrates upon one object, and that, alas, not the Earth-goddess!

He neglects her. Although this happens again and again, this severance with Mother Earth, these times when he abandons her, becomes a wanderer, or hives in great cities, living by the cunning of the mind, we can only guess the reason.

Reticence about any of his deviating lapses that might invalidate his reputation for consistency (not so much his reputation for virtue as his claim of always being in the right) is, as we know, one of Man's primary characteristics. He is not prone to extenuate; he prefers light-heartedly to drop the veil. We may rummage vainly through his historic past for the answer. There is none. We can only imagine. Perhaps he tires of the rôle of hero, or tires of the insistent demand of the Earth-goddess to produce, to work mightily, wearies of the eternal conflict with her and with all nature . . .

He wearies, tires of her . . . That alone we know.

He forgets her—forgets all the old nature gods, except one. Drifting to cities, brain pitted against brain, Man becomes absorbed, enthralled with the trickeries, the subtle and intricate witcheries of the god of commerce.

It is now, too, that disdaining all further allegiance to Mother Earth, freed from her control, he goes in for innumerable cults; serpent worship, tree worship, phallic worship, indulges in secret vices, prostitutes and debases the old symbols, has soft dalliance with Venus the goddess of love, more and more dalliance with other goddesses, with all women, with men . . .

He weakens, becomes flabby, dissolute, corrupt . . . And then one of those periodic displacements, that all the old religions were created to prevent, occurs. There are many contributing causes, no doubt. Mercury is also the god of thieves—but here again persistent silence! We can only conjecture.

It may have been the sky woman who disputes with him his supremacy. Was she not everlastingly advising and scolding Zeus? Or the moon-goddess who, shining by reflected light and feeling that the power of the sun is waning, demands a place in the sun. Perhaps a more clinging and seductive goddess becomes so enamoured with him that she pleads to have a place by his side and to please her he yields. Perhaps, perhaps it is himself! Who or what persuades him is of small matter. The important thing is that the sun's doors have swung open to her, and with a fanfare of trumpets the negative principle, the generic Woman enters in to take her place by man's side. All his goddesses and many other women whom he knows not at all are there. . . .

All except the Earth Woman who remains rooted in what she is—and Venus the goddess of love.

Venus, who never wastes time on women, having plenty of affairs of her own, and who in all her history has never shown the slightest interest in sex solidarity; Venus who does as she pleases, plays her own hand and who knows, moreover, that the sun is a place for burning issues that are more than likely to scorch the wings of Love—Venus does not come.

Once there, triumphantly Woman looks around!

All that has happened is they have changed places. She is out in the full glare of the sun and he automatically retires into the obscurity of the night and reigns in her stead in the pallid moon.

The old legend of the Man in the Moon who was put there as a punishment for picking sticks on Sunday may come in here.

Time goes on. There is unsteadiness. The sun cools, functions erratically. Seasons become mixed, cold summers, warm winters, earthquakes, floods, disasters. The sun is losing its energy, its directive force. There are wars, death, destruction, chaos. . . .

The deserted Earth Mother, the source of all productivity is the most sorrowful figure of all. Desolate, proudly resentful, defiantly she produces gaudy weeds, often beautiful, many times poisonous, a tangled riot of colour, as if to hide her barrenness. Untilled, unharrowed, the tragic earth broods in impenetrable silence. Only the sound of wild beasts is heard. The Earth-goddess reverts to the jungle. Loathsome things prowl over, live with her.

Desolation is abroad. Venus, too, openly mourns that the lack of stability in the sun is affecting the gods who no longer love with the old rapturous ardour, the old endearing masculinity.

Everyone is unhappy—everyone, that is, except Man.

Retired to the cool obscurity of the moon, he has never known such peace. The dream of his life is accomplished—*and respectably*. No one can say he hasn't been fair. He has given her everything she wants. At last, he is eternally divorced from Woman. Here in tranquillity and without Woman he hopes in a life of austere contemplation to end his days. He enjoys meditation when thrust upon him with the same gusto that he enjoys the active life.

It is probable that there will still be emasculated

images of himself strutting about, posing as men. Let them strut, while Man tastes the joys of the monastic life.

After considerable time spent à la Buddha in self-contemplation—the subject is an absorbing one, years could be spent on it and it would not lose in interest—after spending a very, very long time thus happily engaged, he stirs, yawns, stretches, feels his muscle and decides that the moon needs waking up.

The moon rocks with the violence of his energy. It lights up the night with the refulgent glory of the midday sun. Gleeful at this exhibition of the power of Man, he peers over the edge of the moon and catches a glimpse of the Earth woman, sees that she has gone clean to the dogs, forgets the moon, leaps down and takes his place by her side.

She needs him!

She is inescapable, makes all his efforts to do without her vain, and besides, left to herself, she, too, becomes unmoral. She has need of him if only as a dispenser of wisdom—a rôle he greatly enjoys . . . She needs him! She is cold, lifeless, numb. The cord that binds them tightens. He holds her close, close . . .

The wild beasts slink away. The gentler animals come out of hiding, for Man not only is strong but kind. He looks about. The earth has become a shamble, a barren waste. It will take all his furious energy to warm it, to bring back to it the rhythmic beat and throb of life.

"Together!" he whispers to the Earth Mother. Together they will restore the earth, make it to blossom and bring forth fruit. . . .

He mounts to the sun. At his touch the doors open. The imprisoned goddesses, and all the other nondescript women that they had gathered about them, fly out with a loud cry of joy (only the Earth woman likes care, responsibility, work). . . .

"Meditation is all right for a time," Man reflects cheerfully as he steps into the sun and takes his place at the steering wheel, "but, after all, one likes to be the one who keeps things moving."

And equilibrium is once more restored.

Once more he belongs wholly to the Earth woman, the wife, the Great Mother. Not till they two together have brought order again from disorder, have recreated and made beautiful the world, will his roving eyes feel free to look around. Not until bored by the monotony of days, of endless toil that the Earth goddess exacts, hurt by her caprices, her denials, (she is capricious), not till then will he leave her and go off on other pursuits. He will leave her, even though he becomes decadent, corrupt and civilisations fall. . . . *And he will return to her.*

Thus they go on, this inseparable "pair of opposites" always the same.

When you think of the damage, the wanton hurt, you do not wonder that the ancient religions devoted themselves largely to keeping this reckless and irreconcilable pair in order; made use of rite and ritual and magic to propitiate the force of Life; searched earth and sky, sun and moon for symbols of the eternal mating—symbols of the creative power that throbs in everything that lives. The most grotesque and fantastically crude become intelligible and charged with meaning when interpreted as typifying, or as an attribute illustrating the driving force of the creative process. And thus, however wide flung they seem, they may be traced from the rude boundary stones of Hermes, the vulture-headed Hathor, the conical-shaped stones of Venus, the owl vases of Minerva down to the most exquisite statues of the Greeks.

We may marvel over the persistency of these curious signs that have left such an indelible imprint on time; and even were we to ignore their mystical revelation of the august purpose of life, and interpret them on the lower plane of sex, they would still astound, so inexorably do they proclaim that throughout our long history what we are is so precise, so definitely conceived, and what we do to controvert this—may I not say it?—so inept and reasonless.

These two who have been so deeply involved in the rise and fall of civilisations—it is their absolute

difference so marked by these ancient symbols that
dismays while it fascinates the mind. They not only
create life but enter into all the emotions and activi-
ties of life, appearing bracketed together as good
and evil, love and hate, thought and feeling, hunger
and thirst, heat and cold, beginning and end, cause
and effect, concentration and expansion, acquiring
and dispersing, etc., etc. We are advised in the
Bhagavad-Gita to be "free from the 'pair of opposites'," and to "make pain and pleasure, gain and loss,
victory and defeat the same"; yet again it says,
"These two, *light* and *darkness*, are the world's
eternal ways."

We have seen that Man is one being and Woman
many; that he is eternally, terribly active except when
having gone off on a tangent it pleases him to medi-
tate quietly in the moon. He is strong, positive.
Woman is passive, tranquil, non-resistant, and like
the moon shines in a reflected light, the mirror of
what goes on about her. Oblique, obscure in her
processes of thought, when driven into the open she
has a disconcerting way of hitting the exact centre
of the bull's eye—a disconcerting way, too, in an
argument, of letting the subject return on itself
like a circle, no letting up, no stopping, endless!
(The circle is also the symbol of eternity, of perfection, as the dart is the symbol of force, of creative
energy.) Never active until forced by the negligence

of the active principle to stir up disorder, she ends by creating chaos—but only so that order may come again.

The deeper we go into this amazingly complex subject (which can be interpreted in terms of sex, or as spirit and matter, order and disorder, unity and multiplicity—and each is equally true), the more absorbing and enthralling it becomes. Whichever way the adventuring mind goes, if it keeps as Ruskin puts it to the "first narrow thought," many of the puzzling events of the past which have seemed inexplicably irrational, will assume their just proportion and dovetail into a patterned whole—and again the symbolism will be perfect.

If we take it politically, all governments, broadly speaking, have vibrated between these two. Democracy or rule of the people is diffuse, expansive, feminine. Monarchy or rule of the one is strong, positive, masculine. If the masculine preponderates unduly you have a hard, cruel, ruthless civilisation; if the feminine obtains control, repose, passivity degenerate into indolence, weakness, disorder and grossest licentiousness prevails.

Religion, however, has been the greatest battleground for these contending forces that create life. This may be, perhaps, because religion, after all, is merely the manual, the ritual of Life.

In the old Chinese philosophy *Yang*, celestial

breath is pictured as sharing supreme sway with
*Yin*, terrestrial breath and that the alternation of
these two are the cause of growth and decay and the
orderly procedures of nature. This conception ac-
cepts it as the intention that they merge as night and
day in the dawn, and again at sunset, only to fly far
apart, always different, always slightly inimical.

The Buddhist or Taoist conception of immortality
is the ultimate union of the two dualistic forces into
one, thus representing completion instead of negation
or annihilation. This is the ultimate hope, but so
far as we have any records, no matter how old the
civilisation, there has been apparently the same
battle—that still goes on—between positive and
negative, man and woman, spirit and matter or
form.

If we consider in the abstract these creative forces
—man and woman—these "two Regulating Powers
which create by their co-operation all that takes place
in nature," we are able to see how delicate is the
adjustment, how necessary is the union, either by a
Redeemer, a Reconciler, a Mediator or the "higher
third" (Plato called this the child) if life, or knowing
how to live well in the higher sense is the basis of
religion, and also what a part in this development or
collapse both mind and soul play.

It is probable that the conflict between spirit and
matter, positive and negative, man and woman is

perfectly normal, an unremitting vigilance, a sort of sagacious and disciplinary watchfulness that neither shall encroach nor overshadow the other. This is so deeply embedded that it becomes instinctive, really does no harm, keeps each one on guard, sharp-eyed, alert—and extends to idealist and materialist, who while keenly distrustful are mutually dependent on the other.

The old religions whose purpose was to keep the equilibrium, no doubt fostered this, using the symbols of life to keep the thought of balance eternally before men's eyes.

When, however, this battle assumed such gigantic proportions as to throw either force out of line, which it does at times, although far from believing that the soul is always sacrosanct, the trouble presumably has been largely fomented by the mind. Yet it must be understood that the intellect is wholly unaware of this. "The intellect," as Bergson puts it, "so skilful in dealing with the inert, is awkward the moment it touches the living." Mind is naturally arrogant, usurping. Mind and soul are rarely in accord, and both are a little contemptuous of the body. When the soul disdains matter or form, it ends, however, by falling victim to its arch-enemy, the mind. And then we see something like this:—

Intellect takes possession of religion. The soul flees before it. Emotionalism no longer finding its vent in the spiritual, seeks other sources. The old battle between spirit and matter, man and woman, active and passive, now defines itself on the lowest possible plane as one of sex. We have an orgy of it. The emotions, as a matter of fact, have no other outlet but in sex and crime. The old symbols of sex are prostituted and debased as man himself is debased.

When the race itself is endangered we sometimes see intellect that handles life so clumsily driven back to the innocuous quietude of the study by the avenging Great Mother, the great nature goddess and there comes Life—co-operative living once more. More often, the civilisation goes out and another race carries on, using these same symbols. Who can explain?

Man's origin is ever debatable. However it may be accounted for either by fundamentalists or modernists—whether Man came up from a state of bestiality (and the evidences to that end are too remote to affect us except theoretically), or is a fallen angel; history shows remorselessly that periodically he goes through states of bestiality which are termed degeneracy or decadence.

The decline and fall of Rome has been ascribed by historians to various causes—luxury, vice, the destruction of men and wealth by wars, heavy and burdensome taxation, the depreciation of money, irreligion, the infusion of Oriental gods,[1] the Christian religion, the corruption or bad judgment of certain Roman emperors, the trend from the country to the city,[2] (In this connection, it is interesting to note that Jung gives city as a maternal symbol.)[3] While admitting all these to have been factors in the downfall of this once glorious empire, Ferrero stresses as the supreme cause the absence of authority,[4] the flouting of the Senate by the legions, leaving the Empire, without the check of legal procedure, a prey to the whims and passions of mankind, to despotism violent and weak.

This explanation of Ferrero's is quite in line with the symbolism of the dualistic forces. It was simply the old struggle intensified between unity and multiplicity, order and disorder. Disrespect for authority

---

[1] "The religion of the Great Mother (Cybele) with its curious blending of crude savagery with spiritual aspirations, was only one of a multitude of similar Oriental faiths which in the later days of paganism spread over the Roman Empire, and by saturating the European peoples with alien ideals of life, gradually undermined the whole fabric of ancient civilisation." Fraser's *Golden Bough*, abridged edition, p. 357.

"Inoltre, e questo è il colpo di grazia alla civiltà antica, la religione che era stata il fondamento dello Stato è della coltura antica, *il politeismo* agonizza. I culti orientali irrompono dappertutto minacciano di sconvolgere moralmente il mondo." *La Rovina della Civiltà Antica*, G. Ferrero, p. 57.

[2] Ferrero's *La Rovina della Civiltà Antica*, pp. 10, 54, 159.

[3] "The two mother goddesses Rhea and Cybele, both wear the wall crown." Jung's *Psychology of the Unconscious*, p. 334.

*La Rovina della Civiltà Antica*, Ferrero, pp. 32, 37, 39, 123, 187.

is the unmistakable manifestation that order has been defeated by disorder, which in turn, unless conquered, destroys itself.

Fraser quotes from Mommsen that the "rapid diffusion of alien faiths was as much an effect as a cause of widespread intellectual decay. Such unwholesome growths could hardly have fastened upon the Græco-Roman mind in the days of its full vigour."[1]

As man is the primal active force, the conclusion, with no desire to be unfair, must insinuate itself, that in all these extraordinary upheavals that make so much history for us to ponder over, he is the initial offender. In other words, by failing to maintain his supremacy (which consisted in being strong, righteous, everything that is noble and high,) he permitted the forces of anarchy, weakness, disorder to enter in and for this reason it was that the great empire of Rome, once so powerful, crumbled into the dust

Society had rarely been more debased and corrupt than it was in Rome just before the Christian Era. The old religions that had addressed themselves with such grave concern to the stupendous task of preserving the equilibrium between these two that guard the portals of life, had failed or were ignored, and in their place the degenerate Romans had substituted

[1] *Adonis, Attis, Osiris*, Fraser, p. 253. See footnote.

the worship of Cybele and Attis attended by orgiastic rites.[1]

Man had wallowed in the slime of lust and every kind of depravity until he loathed himself. The world rocked with sin. There was no stability anywhere. It was with a sort of desperation, therefore, a mixture of self-disgust and passionate ardour that he embraced a new religion which, casting all the old and futile gods into the dust, responded to the anguished cry of his soul for a way to transcend self.

Even though it eliminated Woman!

His old bitterness, the old, never-ceasing antagonism returned.[2] Was it not Woman with her inordinate desire to give birth that had brought this sorry world into being? Whatever he may have done since, *the world evolved from chaos and chaos was Woman.*

True, there had been a later version. After he had learned to focus himself properly, it was evident that

[1] Gibbon refers to the "licentious tumult of the festival of Cybele." *Decline and Fall of Rome*, Vol. I, p. 114.

[2] Gibbon speaks of the "primitive Roman, who married without love, or loved without delicacy and respect." *Decline and Fall of Rome*, Vol. I, p. 192.

And again "Metallus Numidicus, the censor, acknowledged to the Roman people in a public oration that had kind Nature allowed us to exist without the help of woman we should be delivered from a very troublesome companion; and he could recommend matrimony only as the sacrifice of private pleasure to public duty." *Do.*

he, Man, must have been created before Woman. He had been made by a Great God in His own image. *In the image of God created He him.* Peacefully, happily this first Man walked in a garden of magic beauty, communing as one friend with another with God. Thus Man saw himself! Even in this version however, did not Woman, who arrived later, (created, alas, out of his desire for her!) did she not conspire and cause him to be driven forth from Paradise?

There was exaltation in the thought of denying her. A new way offered itself. Here at last was release.

Was it Balance, though, or was it Flight?

He never paused to ask.

Man became a Christian, austere, a monk.

Even so, he brings all his old symbols of himself and of her (strange creature, Man!) along with him; the cross, circle, dove, eagle, church spire, the tree of life (the Holy Rood), most of the animals that typified creative power or the potency of the Life Force. (His mosaics at Ravenna, and even as late as the cathedral at Ravello show a preponderating use of the old animal and bird motifs.) Of course, too, he brought the triangle, the most omnipotent symbol of all and the one that was to be such a torment to the mediæval theologians![1] Yet they had to have it, had to borrow all these old symbols that have passed from one religion to another. As a

[1] See *Life Symbols.* Chapter on "Triangle," pp. 323–48.

matter of fact they could not do otherwise if they
were to have a religion of Life.

In the present age—an age that has been so wan-
tonly destructive of human life—these old symbols
of life take on a peculiar meaning. Will they be
forced to migrate again, still holding up the torch
that tells us what we are? What will be the next
move—who knows!

And now when we go dreaming to Man's ancient
temples letting the thought of life and its mystery
that makes it forever the quest, envelop us; as we
see these symbols of himself and of Woman, of positive and negative, on all his religious art, if we look
beyond the first narrow interpretation, it brings him
very close to know a little of what he, too, was dreaming, and of his conception of himself as man, and of
woman as woman, (or did it come from on High?)
and of the gods that they two might with impunity
worship, and, most of all, of their own complicated
relationship, that no religion can sever, and no
religion has solved.

# Ancient Pagan Symbols

# Ancient Pagan Symbols

## I.—THE ELEMENTS

REVERENCE for the four elements—fire, water, air,
earth—and the belief that they were a manifestation
of divine power played a large part in many of the
ancient religions. The soul also was thought to be
composed of the four elements, which when united,
took the form of fire or flame. The Egyptians defined
spirit as a "subtle fire," as did the Hindus, who
believed the elements to be eternal, hence the doctrine
that nothing will be annihilated but only changed—
souls by transmigration, matter by transmutation.

The Chinese Taoists, differing from the Greek and
Indian Philosophers, resolved the elements into five:—
water, fire, wood, metal, earth, and believed that
these conquered one another according to a definite
law. Thus wood conquered earth; earth, water;
water, fire; fire, metal; and metal, wood.

Later the Chinese Buddhists adopted the Greek
and Indian idea, adding ether, however, thereby
keeping the number to five.

In this symbolism earth is represented by a square,

water by a circle, fire by a triangle, air by a crescent and ether by a gem—*mani*—the "jewel in the lotus," which surmounts the whole. The mediæval alchemists of Europe adopted practically the same diagram, the

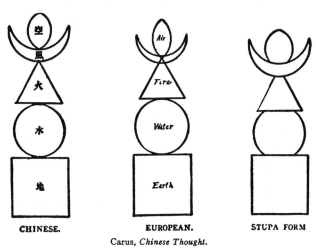

CHINESE.        EUROPEAN.        STUPA FORM

Carus, *Chinese Thought.*

only difference being that they considered the two upper symbols as one and called it air.

This diagram, the *Caitya or Stupa* (*lit.* "precious tower"), may be observed in the open squares of Buddhist monasteries in Japan and Tibet, and in the interior of Asia wherever the influence of the Chinese extends. The symbolism is also depicted on the memorial poles which are placed at the tombs of the dead by the Chinese on their All Soul's Day.

In these "elemental" stupas the square becomes a

cube, the circle a globe, the triangle a four-sided
pyramid, and the moon crescent and linga-shaped
spike are also solid. Placed before monasteries, and
as memorials of those who have passed on, they
convey the suggestion to the living that the body of
the dead has been resolved into its original elements,
and, absorbed in the All, has returned to the origin
and source of all life.

One may conclude, too, that the position of the
elements in the diagram was far from being a hap-
hazard one. The circle (water) stands between the
triangle (fire) and the square (earth), and we shall
have occasion later on to refer to the mystical as well
as practical association of water with earth (matter)
and fire (spirit).

Triangular temples supported by four columns
symbolised, according to Lajard, that the divinity
adored in the Temple was clothed in triple form and
presided over the four elements, which are the agents
of creation and reproduction, or in other words the
four that sustain the created world. Thus Venus
everywhere was queen of three worlds, Heaven,
Earth, Hell and the four elements were among her
attributes, and the numbers three, four and seven
were sacred to her.

## II.—THE LOTUS

*"The flower that was in the Beginning, the glorious lily of the great Water."*

LOTUS, WOR-
SHIPPER AND
WINGED SOLAR
DISK.

Assyrian seal.

As the world was conceived to have come into being by the inter-action of the two elements *fire* and *water*, the **Lotus,** a growth of the watery element, nourished by the rays of the Sun was the symbol *par excellence* of the "spirit moving upon the face of the waters." And its use as a symbol of creation or the beginning of life, goes back beyond the measurements of time.

Its connection, too, with the sun is one of the most ancient traditions of the Egyptian and Hindu mythologies and the one most tenaciously held and preserved. It seems, however, to have been regarded more as the solar matrix than as a symbol of the Sun itself. It was the "mysterious sanctuary," the place where the Sun renewed itself.

In the myth of the Egyptian Horus he is depicted as the new born Sun rising from a lotus flower expanding its leaves on the breast of the primeval deep.

"Brahma springs from the lotus which in its turn rises from the navel of Vishnu."

Brahma is frequently represented as floating on the waters supported by a lotus leaf.

In the Hindu cosmogony the world is likened to a lotus flower floating in the centre of a shallow vessel, which rests on the back of an elephant and the elephant on the back of a tortoise.

LOTUS SUPPORTING WINGED SOLAR DISK.
From a cylinder shown in Lajard, *Culte de Mithra*.

Symbolising solar renascence, the **Lotus** became also a symbol of human re-birth. And thus its association with the doctrine of a future life explains its use in a mortuary way. It appears on the sepulchral tablets of the ancient Greeks and Romans, and was thus employed in early Christian art as an emblem of immortality.

Among the Buddhists the **Lotus** was the emblem of Nirvana. Its mysterious growth, rising from stagnant water and ooze into perflect flower, gloriously unsullied, typified the future possibilities of the human soul, just as its expanded flower resting upon the surface of the placid waters prefigured its ultimate repose after all desire has fled.

The **Lotus** not only typified life, immortality, fecundity, the feminine principle, but also, like the scarabæus, serpent and palm tree, was worshipped as an androgynous symbol of self-creation.

**LOTUS PEDESTAL.**
Supporting the throne of the Master between two Naga Kings.
D'Alviella, *Migration of Symbols.*

Thus as every Buddha and Bodhisattva is self-created and self-existent the **Lotus flower** support typifies his divine birth.

Upon the creation of the world Adi-Buddha the first Buddha was said to have revealed himself on Mount Sumeru in the form of a **Flame**[1] issuing from

---

[1] God appeared to Moses as a flame of fire.

a **Lotus flower.**   In Nepal the Buddha is always represented by this symbol (the union of fire and water).

The Mantra *"Om, mani, padme, hum"*—the jewel
(of creation) is in the lotus—is used in the Yoga
system to express the union of the Two Parts, the
entire system being founded upon the union of Spirit
and Matter.

The phallic significance of the "jewel in the lotus"
is, of course, obvious.

The **Lotus** is sometimes depicted with a **Moon
crescent** above it.

LOTUS AND THE MOON-GOD.
Assyrian Seal.
Goodyear, *Grammar of the Lotus.*

The **Flame** symbol rising from the centre of a moon
crescent which we first see in the diagram of the
elements will be encountered again and again.   Its
shape changes slightly, it is known under various
names, but whether the flame rests in the moon
crescent or in the lotus it typifies the union of the
dualistic forces that create life, the "jewel" indicating
the masculine principle and the lotus or moon crescent
the feminine, while the bursting seed pods symbolise
fecundity.

The **Lotus** as an attribute of Osiris, who was the Egyptian God of the Resurrection, or the Sun at night had a three-fold significance symbolising the Sun, the resurrection and creative force and power.

The **Lotus** is given to Isis in her character of goddess of fecundity.

In the Christian religion the **Lotus** becomes the Lily of the Virgin, and is given to certain saints to emphasise the purity of their lives.

The ancients who did nothing in a meaningless way, and in all their art expressions testified to their profound worship of Life made elaborate use of the leaves, buds and flowers of the lotus as decorative motifs. The capitals on the majority of the Egyptian columns represented a lotus flower with the upper part cut off.

The **Lotus** is the **Wheel** symbol of Buddha, the petals representing spokes and the whole typifying the doctrine of perpetual cycles of existence.

The **Rosettes** so frequently found as architectural ornaments have been traced back by scholars to the lotus, and thus take on a solar significance.

The **Anthemion** or honeysuckle design so much used by the Greeks, was found on the earliest monuments of Nineveh. It was evidently an object of religious worship there, and owes its origin to the lotus bud, the supremely sacred flower.

Goodyear attributes the **Egg and dart** motif, still

# Ancient Pagan Symbols

ASSYRIAN WINGED DEITIES FACING ROSETTE.
Bas-relief from Khorsabad.

used by architects, to the lotus. And one may assume
without much questioning that this and similar modes
of ornamentation that present a rhythmic use of the
upright and curve, may be traced back to the "jewel
in the lotus" or the conjunction of the Divine pair.

DETAIL OF CYPRIAN VASE SHOWING LOTUS AND SWASTIKAS.
Metropolitan Museum of Art.

The **Lotus** is called the Flower of Light—flower de luce, *fleur de lys*. As the latter it is the emblem of France. It is the Florentine lily. It was used to symbolise the Trinity, Christ as the "Light of the World that dispels all darkness" was symbolised by the *fleur de lys*.

"When Buddha was born a lotus bloomed where he first touched the ground; he stepped seven steps northward and a lotus marked each footfall."

## III.—THE TREE OF LIFE

SACRED TREE TERMINATING IN
LOTUS BUDS OR PINE CONES.
Layard, *Nineveh*.

To the ancients who sought to find in nature the secret of life nothing was a more perfect symbol of the miracle of reproduction than the tree with its leaves and blossoms and fruit. Those that shed their leaves in autumn only to put forth in tenderest green in the spring conveyed the divine assurance of renewal, of "dying to live" which was the frame work of the old religions. On the other hand, the trees that remained always green symbolised the everliving spirit, green typifying the everlasting. Thus the **Cypress** reaching toward heaven like a pointed flame, the **Pine Tree** from its resemblance to a spiral of flame, the straightness and uprightness of the **Pine** and **Fir** and the fact that they were continually green made them symbolic figures of highest import only surpassed, perhaps, by the **Palm.**

The belief was wide spread that the **Pine** and **Cypress,** because of their greater vitality, had the power to strengthen the soul of the deceased and to preserve his body from corruption. Hence their use in cemeteries.

The **Pine Cone** from its inflammable nature (fire wherever found being a potent attribute of the primary creative force) was used as a phallic emblem. Among the Semites, however, it came to have a deeper meaning, and like the *crux ansata* of the Egyptians typified an existence united yet distinct

Tree terminating in the Sacred Cone protected by birds and lions.
From the Cathedral of Torcello.   D'Alviella.

or the union of the positive and negative forces. The **Sacred Cone** is found constantly on Assyrian monuments, on Etruscan sepulchral urns, and its use spread to the Greeks and Romans. The **Pine Cone** conventionalised and enlarged may still be seen on gateways in Italy as a talisman of abundance, fecundity, good luck. It was also a symbol of Venus and Artemis.

Besides the fact that the **Sacred Tree** varied in different localities, its association with the feminine principle (the tree becoming the symbol of the matrix) is responsible for legend after legend connecting the tree with Astarte, Ishtar, Mylitta and other nature goddesses. Primitive man worshipped the divine Creator in the form of a pyramidal cone or obelisk, and the **Cypress,** possibly because of its pyramidal form, sometimes took the place of the conical stone of Astarte on the coins of Heliopolis. Venus of Lebanon was called the Cypress. An ancient altar has a solar god on one side and on the other a **Cypress** that has a child with a ram on its shoulder peeping out from its foliage. It is in a **Pine** that Cybele imprisons the body of Attis the spring time god. And Attis was said to have met his death by self-mutilation under a sacred tree. Adonis sprang from a tree. In the legend of Osiris the body of Osiris is concealed in the branches of a tamarisk bush which, enclosing the body, suddenly shot-up into a marvellously beautiful tree. In the Northern mythology the All Father is identified with **Yggdrasil the Mighty Ash** whose roots were in the well of wisdom, ("wisdom is a tree of life to them that lay hold of her"), and beneath whose branches the gods met in daily council.

The sap or life principle in trees was believed to have been derived from the "Creative tears of the gods." Thus the living tree as the receptacle of divine

life was doubtless placed near pillars in the cult of
pillar and stone worship, with the thought of assisting
or bearing witness to the divine life in stock and stone.
**Birds** are a feature of tree worship, the divine essence
descends on tree or pillar or stone in the form of a bird.
And, however widely scattered the countries, wherever
trees were worshipped the **Serpent** appears, either

SERPENT IN BACKGROUND.
Chaldean cylinder.   British Museum.
Perrot and Chipiez.

lifting its head in the background or coiled about the
sacred tree.

Both the Aryan and Semitic races had a **Tree of
Life,** a **Tree of Knowledge** and a **Tree of Heaven.**

After Adam and Eve are driven forth for partaking
of the tree of knowledge of good and evil, the Lord
places "at the east of the garden of Eden cherubim
and a flaming sword which turned every way, to keep
the way of the tree of life."

It is the **Tree of Life** that is so jealously guarded.

The **Haoma** whose sap gave immortality was the
traditional **Tree of Life** of the Persians.   This is the

**Cosmic Tree** which produces ambrosia and dispenses salvation, and is identified with the **Soma** so celebrated in the Rig-veda. The juice of the sacred plant was drunk sacramentally, it was the libation of the gods, the draught of immortality and fills with religious fervour and ecstasy the hearts of those who drink of it. It gives strength and courage, and the Vedic god Indra partakes of it nightly before going forth to conquer the dragon Vritra. So potent is it that Soma the drink of the gods, which moves and inspires them to high deeds, is itself hailed as a god possessed of divine power.

The *Sien* trees of the Chinese are those that confer health, strength, life, immortality, such as the jejube, plum, pear, peach—any tree, in short, that produces fruit—or aromatic or edible matter.

Fruits of the vine or tree yielded by fermentation a liquid that is still called *Eau de vie.*

The Chinese **Tree of Life,** was one of seven marvellous trees that grew on the slope of the Kuen-Luën Mountains, the terrestrial paradise presided over by Si Wang Mu. The fruit of this tree was supposed to be the **Sacred Peach** which entered so largely into the mysticism of the Taoists, who used the **peach tree** as a symbol of marriage, longevity, immortality. Anyone to whom the Chinese goddess gave the fruit became immortal. In Chinese art Si Wang Mu is symbolised by a **peach** and a **phoenix.**

The **Sacred Tree** in Japan is the *Sa-ka-ki* tree. In the various ceremonies in the temples, branches of the *Sa-ka-ki* tree to which are attached a mirror, a sword and a jewel are among the offerings.

The American Indian had a **World Tree** and the Five Nations always expressed peace under the metaphor of a tree. The Senal Indians of California believed that the earth was once a globe of fire, and that that element passing up into the trees, came out again when two pieces of wood were rubbed together. The Delaware myth of the World Tree features it as springing from the back of a tortoise. This resembles the Hindu myth of the tortoise who supports the world.

The Aryans of Europe worshipped the **Oak** which was sacred to the gods of fertility and thunder. In Greece and Italy Zeus and Jupiter were oak-gods. One of the oldest modes of divination seems to have been that of interpreting the voices of the wind sighing in the tops of the oak trees. In Dodona, a famous sanctuary in Greece, Zeus was worshipped in the oracle giving oak, from whose roots a perpetual spring flowed. As a rain charm it was customary for the priest of Zeus to dip an oak branch into a sacred spring. As the oak was pre-eminently symbolical of fire, we have here once more the union of **fire** and **water** as agents of productivity, which as will be seen

again and again, play such an important part in the
worship of primitive peoples.

**Fire** kindled by lightning was looked upon with
superstitious awe. God himself spoke in the thunder
and lightning. As the **Oak** appears to have been
struck oftener than other trees, the ancients believed
that the great sky-god loved it better than any tree in
the world. The **Oak** was sacred to the Druids, and
Frazer suggests that the reason why they worshipped a
mistletoe bearing oak was the belief that the mistletoe
"descended from the sun in a flash of lightning," and
that the oak thus bore among its branches a "visible
emanation of the celestial fire." [1] The mistletoe,
growing without roots in the ground, evergreen
when the oak was barren and lifeless, was worshipped
as imperishable, and became one of those mystical
emblems of life and immortality from which countless
inferences, myths and customs have been derived.

The **Oak** from its association with fire seems to have
been considered masculine.

In the worship of Diana in her sacred grove at
Nemi a perpetual fire was kindled and fed by the
sacred oak and cared for by Vestal Virgins.

The primitive method of producing fire was by the
friction of two pieces of wood, usually of oak. Oak
ignited in this way was used by the ancient Celts,
Germans and Slavs to kindle the **Beltane** and **Mid-**

[1] Fraser's *The Golden Bough*, abridged edition, p. 710.

**summer Fires** which were annual fire festivals and the
**Need Fires** which were resorted to in times of distress.
The **Yule log** so long a feature of Christmas festivities
was also of oak.[1]

Long before he came to build temples primitive
man worshipped his gods in the open, on high
places, and in natural woods. The marriage of Jupiter
and Juno as oak-god and oak-goddess was celebrated
annually by the early Romans in a sacred grove of
oaks. In certain parts of Greece also the sacred
marriage of Zeus and Hera as oak-god and goddess
was celebrated each year with great religious pomp
and ritual. Later the gods were impersonated by
kings and queens crowned with oak leaves and later
still these ceremonies, pure in their inception, performed as magical rites to propitiate the fructifying
powers of nature, degenerated into wild orgies as
notorious as they were indecent.

The **Sacred Fig Tree**—*ficus religiosa*—combining
both masculine and feminine attributes was held in
especial veneration as an emblem of life in all countries
bordering on the southern shores of the Mediter-
ranian. Its tri-lobed leaf, suggesting the masculine
triad became the symbolic covering in statues of the
nude, while the fruit—the eating of which was supposed to aid fecundity—was identified in shape with
the *yoni*.

[1] See *Life Symbols*, pp. 186–93.

"In the forum, the busy centre of Roman life, the sacred fig tree of Romulus was worshipped down to the days of the empire, and the withering of its trunk was enough to spread consternation through the city." [1]

Every Buddha had a **Bo-Tree** or **Bodhi-Tree,** the Tree of Wisdom or Enlightenment under which he is supposed to have been born, do penance, preach and die.

Although some have pictured it as the **Banyan Tree,** it is the **Fig Tree**—*ficus religiosu*—that is usually represented as the one under which Gautama Buddha receives *bodhi* or knowledge.

The **Palm Tree,** the only tree known to the ancients that never changed its leaves, was classed with the lotus, serpent and scarabæus as self-created and self-sustaining and therefore held in highest veneration as typifying the miracle of reproduction.

Thus the **Palm,** used by the Christians as a symbol of martyrdom (although it may easily have had a deeper meaning—the triumph of life over death), was an ancient androgynous or bi-sexual symbol of creative force, or the generating power of nature. And in Chaldea, Assyria and Babylonia the symbolical tree of Life found its highest expression in conventional representations of the **Date Palm.**

The **Assyrian Tree of Life** is probably the oldest, as

[1] Fraser's *The Golden Bough*, abridged edition, p. 111.

it is the most famous of all sacred trees, and it still
gives definite form to various ornamental designs.
Starting in Assyria where it seems to have been
associated with the worship of Venus (or Ishtar) it
penetrated into Arabia, Central Asia, Asia Minor and
Persia.

SACRED TREE SHOWING DIVIDED PILLAR.
Layard, *Monuments of Neneveh.*

It first appears on Chaldean cylinders as a pillar or
"World Spine" surmounted by a crescent, frequently
the pillar is thrice-crossed by branches which end in
circles. About the beginning of the tenth century
B.C. the tree becomes more complex. Conventionalised into elaborate and graceful forms, it was one of

the most conspicuous objects found on the sculptures
and monuments of Khorsabad and Nimroud.

From the "mystic flower of the Assyrians," which
Goodyear identifies with the lotus, innumerable
branches spring from an intricate scroll-work or
interlacing design. The pillar or trunk of the tree is
sometimes divided, suggesting the same idea of
duality, or union of spirit and matter that is conveyed

ASSYRIAN CYLINDER.

by the bird and serpent. (In all countries, as we have
seen, the serpent was invariably associated with the
Tree of Life, the bird typifying spirit or soul also
constantly appears.) Whether the branches terminate
in the lotus bud, pomegranate, or sacred cone, the
fruit of the tree is never other than one of the well
known symbols of life or fecundity.

To indicate the high significance of the tree as a
religious emblem the winged circle of the deity is
frequently placed above it.

The **Sacred Tree** is often represented between two unicorns or two winged bulls or two oxen with eagle heads; again a wild goat or sacred bull kneels before it; it is shown between two kings who stand in an attitude of worship; sometimes it is between two priests, two winged females are also depicted with one hand extended toward the tree and the other holding the ring or circle, symbol of eternity, water, the feminine principle.

FROM ATHENS CATHEDRAL.

These animals or winged figures are considered to be the guardians of the sacred tree. And although occasionally the two fabulous beasts are portrayed as if about to pluck the fruit, the essential character of the myth seldom varies.

One can only touch upon some of these innumerable forms, all of which seem to have been used to convey

URN, FIFTH CENTURY
(Mausoleum of Galla Placidia, Ravenna.)

URN OF ARCHBISHOP THEODORE
(S. Apollinare in Classe, Ravenna.)

Photo, Alinari

BYZANTINE URN
(S. Apollinare in Classe, Ravenna.)

Photo, Alinari

URN
(S. Apollinare in Classe, Ravenna.)

one of the most profound and persistent associations in ancient religious belief—the union of fire and water, positive and negative, masculine and feminine, spirit

PHŒNICIAN BOWL.

and matter as the consecrated channels through which the Life Force flows.

The Buddhists depict the **Sacred Tree** between two elephants. Sometimes the tree dwindles into the mystic flower of the lotus, flanked by the same two elephants. The connection is obvious. The lotus was called the Tree of Life of Mazdaism.

The Phœnicians used the same form. In this case it appears to be the conventionalised lotus.

D'Alviella, *Migration of Symbols.*

It is worth noting that in all these representations, no matter how fantastic the form, the symbolic idea of life is always conveyed. And also, even when the tree is replaced by some other symbolic object the grouping does not alter.

Sometimes an altar or pyre takes the place of the tree. In China the tree becomes the **Sacred Pearl** between two dragons.

The Phrygians depicted lions, bulls or winged sphinxes facing each other, and between them they placed the phallus or sacred pillar or an urn.

The Christians in making use of this ancient symbolic form sometimes depicted the two figures as lambs or again as doves or peacocks.

The **Tree of Life** becomes the genealogical tree, the family tree, the tree of Jesse. The latter showing the genealogy of Christ is found in the Jesse windows in mediæval churches.

CAPITAL OF THE TEMPLE OF ATHENE AT PRIENE.

## IV.—THE DUAL PRINCIPLES

*"There are in life two elements, one transitory and progressive, the other comparatively if not absolutely non-progressive and eternal."*—Gilbert Murray.

LYCIA.

D'Alviella.

THE Hindus gave the name of the "pair of opposites" to the dual aspect of nature which manifests itself as sun and moon, light and darkness, heat and cold, fire and water, man and woman, day and night, etc.

From remotest times **Man,** the active principle has been symbolised by fire, by whatever is pointed, direct—a spear, shaft, column, dart, arrow, the "Rod of Jesse." And **Woman,** the feminine or passive principle by water, by everything that is sinuous, concave, curving, receptive—by the earth, by mounds, high places, mountains, by the moon, air, crescent, pearl—by whatever is hollow, oval, cavernous, circular, a receptacle.

The **red** of fire typified the masculine principle and the **blue** of the sea the feminine. The sea was looked

upon as the Great Mother of all things. From the
agitation of the primordial waters life (which was
motion) began to be. Out of darkness and death
came light and life. Night was parent of the day.
This was shown also in the Hebrew account of creation.
Until the movement of the Spirit upon the waters,
all was darkness and chaos. The belief in a Saviour
God born of a Virgin, often named Maria or some
name meaning *mare*—sea—seems to have obtained
among many of the ancient races. The association of
**Woman** with **Water** has been given an esoteric
interpretation. **Water** is conceived of as the "connecting link between Spirit or pure thought and Matter
or concrete form. . . . This is the Cosmic Element
which is esoterically called 'Water'."[1]   Thus water
the intermediary or "Distributive Medium" between
spirit and matter typified woman, the soul, the
psychic side of man, the mother of individual life.

The **Circle** has always symbolised eternity, that
which is without beginning or end; it is also one of
the symbols of water or the passive principle of life.
The use of **Water** as a sacrament of regeneration,
symbolising spiritual re-birth goes back to earliest
times, and the figure eight formed of two circles enters
into the mystery of numbers. The baptismal fonts
in Christian churches were octagonal in form, thus
signifying that creation having been completed in

[1] Troward's *Bible Mystery and Bible Meaning*, pp. 14-15.

seven days, eight figured regeneration, the beginning anew. The symbolism of the octave also enters in here.

The **Circle** typified the eternal continuity of life and from this may have come about the custom of reckoning time by circlets of beads.

The **Rosary** as an aid in repeating mystical sentences was used in the Eastern religions. Ivory, jade and crystal beads, also those carved from the wood of the plum and cherry trees were used by the Buddhists.

The **Circle** also denotes perfection, the Perfect One, the Pearl of Price.

The **Ark** is one of the most sacred and universal symbols of the feminine or passive principle.

The **Pole** is a derivative of a Phœnician word which means "he breaks through" or "passes into." Pillars, obelisks, columns, monoliths and shafts are all of phallic origin, and as symbols of creative energy were objects of reverential worship among all ancient races. Church spires are a relic of the same primitive symbolism of creative force.

The **Pillar** is constantly referred to in the Bible as a symbol of the Creator.

The **Sacred Pole** or **Asherah** of the Hebrews probably belongs to the same symbolism of life and reproduction that is expressed in the Old Testament by Aaron's rod (Num. 17:8) and also by the Rod or Stem of Jesse (Isa. 11:1).

The **Pillar** or **Dolmen** is continually linked with sacred trees, and the association forms a part of Druidical worship.

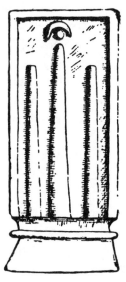

CARTHAGINIAN PILLAR SHRINE ON STELE, NORA, SARDINIA.
The moon-spirit was believed to inhabit the lunar stone.
Evans, *Mycenæn Trees and Pillar Cult.*

In the cult of Asherah it might be either a living tree or an artificially constructed pole or post before which the Canaanites placed their altars.

The **Tower** is an outgrowth of the pillar and the **Round Towers** of Ireland, supposed by some to have been built by Persian refugees, and attributed by others to the Gynosophists, a society founded on

Buddhism and driven out of India by the **Brahmins**, probably belonged to this form of worship.

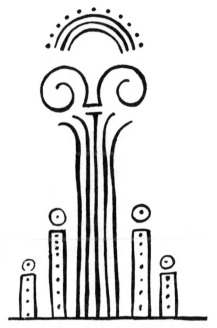

A **Staff** supporting a semi-circle is one of the earlier forms of pillar worship in Cyprus and Chaldea. The *Staff* is the battle standard of Ashur, Tammuz and Osiris who were tree gods as well as vegetation gods. The **Staff of Life** is frequently depicted on ancient gems, coins and sculpture.

To show their divine origin a raised sun disk is often portrayed with these pillars or shafts.

Egyptian religious art conveyed the same thought by the two uracus serpents curving up either side of a pole or pillar. This, too, is one of those immortal designs, used to symbolise the Life impulse, whose antiquity only makes its future more sure.

The classic form of the **Caduceus,** a winged rod entwined by two serpents, was originally a rod— believed to be the **Sacred Tau**—surmounted by a circle upon which rests a crescent. It was the emblem of life and power, and Mercury always bore the caduceus when conducting the souls of the dead.

The **Crosier** and **Shepherd's Crook** are offshoots of this symbolism. The crosier was supposed to have been a tau cross and was not given its bent appearance until the seventeenth century.

Osiris in judging the dead is represented as holding in his hands "the crook, the sceptre and the flail, emblems of rule, sovereignty and dominion."

The **Sceptre,** derived from the divided pillar or pillar with a globular break in the middle, was used in the dual cult to typify the union of the two creative forces, and from the most ancient days was a symbol of royal power given only to kings and rulers, and the great gods and goddesses of life.

The same simplicity of thought must have led to the blending of the two colours which symbolised

Man and Woman, the red of fire and the blue of the sea—which thus became the imperial purple, the royal insignia of power worn by the Roman Emperors.

The combination of **Upright and Circle**—"I the 'Holy One,' the Pole or Axis of the universe," and O—*eau*—water, the Perfect One, the Divine Receptacle, has been one of the most prolific sources of sacred forms and ideas.

The Maoris are said to worship a First Cause under the name of Io.

The decade 10 is a combination of upright and circle and was interpreted by Pythagoras as forming, as it were, a monad with which re-commences a new series capable of infinite expansion.

The **Maypole** and its ring is a survival of some ancient springtime festival where men did honour to the mysterious reciprocal powers of nature.

In this symbolism of **Pole** and **Circle** the dominant, forceful upright was looked upon as Creator, and the circle was the "regulator or bridle of time and motion." One sees here also the esoteric connection between the circle and the tides of the sea.

This ancient conception of the active and passive principles of life as angular and curved has formed the basis of many of the most beautiful and elaborate designs that have been bequeathed to us from an immemorial past.

**Two Pillars** signifying strength and beauty symbolised the gateway to Eternity.

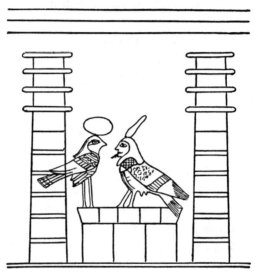

ENTRANCE TO TATTU IN AMENTA.

Showing the two Tat Pillars, and Ra the God in Spirit, and Osiris who is God in the Body or Mummy-form.

Churchward, *Signs and Symbols of Primordial Man.*

It was an ancient Babylonian belief that the sun-god re-enters the inhabited world each morning between **Two Pillars**. Thus it was customary to place two pillars in the Semitic Temples.

**Two Pillars** guarded the entrance to Solomon's Temple, one the "Stablisher" and the other "In it is strength." (II. Chron. 3: 17.)

A **Pair of Obelisks** in front of Egyptian temples, often preceeded by long avenues of sphinxes or rams, conveyed the same idea as the huge phalli in the Eastern religions. They typified strength, protection against evil influences.

The traditional sanctity of doorways, portals, gateways is well known, and these with their two pillars are frequently pictured with the sacred tree.

SYRIA.

The two opposite forces were also represented as twin horsemen, the "primeval twins."

The "Twin Brother Idea," one of whom envies and slays the other, appears constantly under various names, Osiris and Set, Baldur and Loki, Cain and Abel, Jacob and Esau—and has been interpreted as a dramatic version of the old struggle between light and darkness, good and evil, or the positive and negative forces of life.

Among all ancient races **Rocks** and **Stones** were worshipped as symbols of the Creator. Hence arose the belief in the magical and medicinal qualities, in the luck and ill luck that is still attached to certain precious stones. The custom of wearing charms or amulets is a relic of stone worship.

**MITHRA BORN FROM THE ROCK.**

His head is adorned with a Phrygian cap. He has a dagger in one hand and a lighted torch in the other.

Bas-relief found in the Crypt of St. Clements at Rome. Cumont, *Mysteries of Mithra.*

The word rock has been identified with fire. Thus "Mithra was said to have been born of a rock, to have wedded a rock, and to have been the parent of a rock."

**Altars** and **Rocks** were modified forms of pillars; the rock a simplification of the pillar and the altar a place of offering. In the early religions of Northern India the first sacrifice was to Mother Earth, the feminine manifestation of creative energy. The altar, a heaped-up mound of earth symbolised the sacred mother. This altar not only was the earth but the earth as woman. The first altars among the Jews were also of earth.

Later these altars became slabs for votive offerings and were placed over the pillar shrines which were slightly conical in form. The posts added for security gave rise to a table form and to certain types of tripod. The **Mothers** according to the Pelasgians were identical with the tripod upon which and inside of which they lived.

**Rocks, Stones, Altars** and **Pillars** are constantly referred to in the Old Testament as symbols of the Creator. Among the Druids, as we have seen, the stone pillar or menhir was associated with tree worship. In the primitive religions of India the same custom prevailed of setting up sacred stones beneath their holy trees. The Egyptians perpetuated the worship of trees, wells, stones and mounds and called precious stones "hard stones of truth."

Swedenborg made precious stones the symbol of spiritual truths.

This same symbolism was displayed in primitive temples, which were made of **Circles of Stones** in the centre of which was kindled the **Sacred Fire.**

This circular space was sometimes enclosed in a

**Square.** A **Square Stone** was used by the Arabians and the Greeks of early days as a symbol of Venus or the feminine principle. A **Square** on Greek coins and Egyptian amulets contains different symbols of the Deity, sometimes the sun disk with rays, thus carrying out the old symbology of the sun and earth.

The Egyptians put green stone amulets in their tombs as symbols of everlasting youth and immortality. Horus, the morning sun, who typified eternal youth, was called the "Prince of the Emerald Stone."

Among the ancient Chinese **Jade** was the most precious mineral and was always identified in their philosophy with Heaven. Certain things like jade and gold were believed to be imbued with vital energy derived from the great *yang* element, or divine creative energy which they called Heaven. This is indestructible, hence its symbols must also be indestructible. "Heaven is jade, is gold."

SICILIAN BAS-RELIEF.
D'Alviella, *Migration of Symbols.*

## V.—THE CROSS

MONOGRAM OF CHRIST. LABARUM OF CONSTANTINE.

**The Cross,** its origin unknown, comes to us out of the misty past as a supremely sacred symbol.

**The Cross** is found among the most sacred hieroglyphics of Egypt. It appears thus ✕ (still used as a sign of multiplication), and thus + (the plus sign) and again thus **T**—the **Sacred Tau.** And constantly repeated on all the old Egyptian remains, one sees a figure like this ☥. This is known as the *Crux Ansata*, the Egyptian Ankh, the Key of the Nile, the Key of Life or the Cross of Egypt. Peculiarly

MALTESE CROSS.

identified with Egypt, yet it is found as a religious emblem among all the other races of antiquity.

The meaning attached to the *crux ansata*—also implied by the simpler cross—is "Life to Come."

The **Cross** has lent itself to a great variety of forms— the Greek cross, the Latin cross, the Maltese cross,

GREEK CROSS.

etc.—and to almost as many interpretations. It has been called the cosmic symbol of the four quarters of the earth, or the four cardinal points. The Greek Cross represented the winds from the four quarters. The American Indians used it to typify the winds which bring rains. The Aztec goddess of rain held a cross in her hand.

The **Tau Cross** was considered a divine symbol by

MEXICAN SACRED TREE.
D'Alviella, *Migration of Symbols.*

the ancient Mexicans, who called it the Tree of Life, Tree of our Flesh, Tree of Nutriment. It was later consecrated to the god of rain, and in these representations was frequently given a tree-like form or that of a stem with two branches. Sometimes a bird is depicted standing upon the fork.

**Thor's Hammer** is said to have been the Tau. As Thor was a sky god, a thunder god, his hammer was a symbol of rain and fertility, hence power. It has been likened also to the fylfot cross (swastika), and the Chinese Y. Like the thunderbolt in the hands of the Assyrian storm gods it was a weapon of divine power.

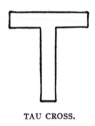

TAU CROSS.

The **Cross** has been associated with the *crossed fire sticks* of the Chinese, it has been likened to a bird with outstretched wings, to two human figures crossed, and to man himself standing with outstretched arms. Interpreted in the latter sense as symbolising the divine potential Man—we can understand why criminals were nailed to the cross, the symbol which they had profaned; and why a man who cannot write still signs his name with a cross.

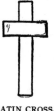

LATIN CROSS.

Thus interpreted the symbolism of the cross with circle above it ceases to be a mystery. It represented quite simply the union of spirit and matter, masculine and feminine, and has been used as an emblem of life and immortality since prehistoric days. It is given to the Egyptian deities. Maat, the goddess of Truth, is

CRUX ANSATA.

depicted presenting it to the Sun, the source of all life, and placed on tombs and sarcophagi it signified the ever living spirit, the immortality of the soul.

The **Cross** with a wheel in the centre is one of the

oldest symbols of majesty and power in India and
was given to Vishnu.

A glance at the astronomical signs, which are said
to have originated with the Egyptians, shows the
cross, circle and crescent variously posed; that of
Venus, the cross surmounted by a circle, is the old
symbol of fecundity or life, and that of Mercury the
older form of his caduceus, the Sacred Tau surmounted by the circle and crescent.

DETAIL OF CYPRIAN VASE.
(Metropolitan Museum of Art.)

## VI.—THE SERPENT

*"It is fate itself, swift as disaster, deliberate as retribution, incomprehensible as destiny."*

NĀGA KINGS SUP-
PORTING THE
LOTUS PEDESTAL.

D'Alviella, *Migra-
tion of Symbols.*

No symbol is more frequently met with in ancient religious art, and none has so contradictory a meaning. It typifies wisdom, power, life, reproduction, eternity; it is also associated with everything low, base, dark, evil. It is one of the universal attributes of the creative principle. It is common to both elements, earth and water, is closely connected with groves and tree worship, and from earliest times was an inseparable feature of sun worship.

The fact that the **Serpent** was believed to be androgynous added to its reverence. Its annual sloughing of its skin made it a symbol of being born anew.

The **Serpent** with tail in its mouth forming a circle, was an Egyptian symbol of eternity and immortality.

It was the emblem of destruction, death. "As the

worm of corruption it is the mightiest of all adversaries of the gods."

Typifying darkness it is the enemy of the gods of light, who are represented in mortal combat with the serpent of evil and darkness.

**LIBATION VASE OF GREEN STONE.**
Jastrow, *Civilisation of Babylonia and Assyria.*

**Serpents** were worshipped as defenders of households. Snake charms, snake rings, snake bracelets were worn as fertility and protective amulets.

A **Snake** is one of the symbols of Athene, the goddess of wisdom.

Æsculapius, god of medicine and son of Apollo,
carries a staff encircled by a serpent symbolising
healing, the renewing power of life.

Hippocrates is given the same symbol.   Hygeia,
the goddess of health, holds a serpent in her hand.

Vishnu, the preserver of the Hindu Trimurti, sleeps
on the World Serpent's body.

The Serpent is depicted coiled about the Egg of the
World.

The Cross is often entwined by the serpent as a
symbol of spiritual re-birth.


"In the Biblical narrative the sexual instinct and
the beginning of culture as symbolised by the tree
of knowledge are closely associated.   According to
rabbinical traditions the serpent is the symbol of the
sexual passion."[1]

Conceived of as the manifestation of the Life
Principle it symbolises wisdom, power, creation.   In
the negative or evil sense it is the deadly reptile of
materialism and sensuality.   It was the serpent in
this latter aspect that brought about the expulsion of
Adam and Eve from the Garden of Eden.

"The snake in paradise is usually considered
feminine as the seductive principle in woman, and is

[1] Jastrow's *Religion of Babylonia and Assyria.*

ATHENE (MINERVA)
(Vatican, Rome.)

ARES (MARS) IN REPOSE
(Museo Ludovisi Boncompagni, Rome.)

represented as feminine by the old artists, although properly the snake has a phallic meaning."[1]

Its association with earth and water made it a symbol *par excellence* of the feminine or negative principle. Combining both natures, as it was believed, would give it undoubted phallic meaning. Traces have been found of a very early religion in India which embodied the worship of Mother Earth and the Great Snake Father.

The Indian Nāgas or serpent gods were believed to be superior to men.

JAPAN.

Nāga Kings with two dragons on shoulders upholding the lotus pedestal of the god.

D'Alviella, *Migration of Symbols.*

[1] Jung's *Psychology of the Unconscious*, p. 110.

## VII.—THE CHINESE TRIGRAMS

THE GREAT MONAD.   THE TAI-KIH.

THE old Chinese religion was based on the idea that Heaven and Earth — themselves the greatest gods — produce all things by the inter-action of the opposites. From remotest times the Chinese have divided nature into two great parts:—*Yang*, the positive, masculine principle, denotes light, warmth, life. *Yin*, the negative or feminine principle, is darkness, cold, death. *Yang* is the sun, *Yin* the earth. *Yang* is the celestial and *Yin* the terrestrial breath.

The **Great Monad,** the *ovum mundi* of the Chinese, which symbolises the Chinese dualistic philosophy, is a circle divided by two arcs of opposite centres. In this mystic union of the two principles, the dark represents *Yin*, the material or feminine principle, and the light, *Yang*, the spiritual or masculine principle.

A third arc from above is sometimes depicted uniting them. This represents the Tai-Kih, the Great Uniter which as a symbolic figure plays such a great part in the mysticism, divination and decorative art of China.

Brinton interprets this as expressing in "Platonic language the One as distinguished from the Many," and adds that as the Chinese believed in the mystic power of numbers and that that which reduces all multiplicity to unity naturally controls or is at the summit of all things, therefore the Tai-Kih expresses the completest and highest creative force. Thus the universe being made up of opposites was brought into fructifying union by the Tai-Kih. "Abstractly the latter would be regarded as the synthesis of the two universal antitheses which make up all phenomena."[1]

The circle is sometimes divided by three lines resembling the Chinese $Y$, the latter a symbol of vast antiquity. Used in this way it carries the same suggestion.

The symbolism of the inter-action of the famous **Eight Trigrams** is found in the Yi King or Book of Changes. "These trigrams determine good and evil, and good and evil cause the great business of human life."

Everything being produced by *Yang* and *Yin*, the Celestial and Terrestrial Breaths, the outcome for good or ill is in exact mathematical proportion to the way these are combined. The struggle between and different admixtures of these two contrasting, elementary forces make all the conditions that prevail.

[1] *The Ta-Ki, the Svastika and the Cross in America*, D. G. Brinton.

*Yang* is symbolised by a whole line ——— indicating strength.

*Yin* is symbolised by a divided line —— —— indicating weakness.

These lines placed over themselves and each other formed the four Hsiang or Emblematic Symbols.

These same lines placed successively over each other formed the eight Kwa or Trigrams. There are only eight possible combinations of such trigrams, to each

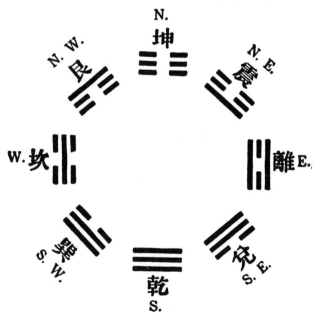

ARRANGEMENT OF TRIGRAMS ACCORDING TO FUH-HI.

of which was assigned a special meaning which formed
the basis of divination.

The two fundamental lines added to each of the
eight trigrams produce sixteen figures of four lines
each. This is carried on to thirty-two figures of five
lines each. A similar addition produces the sixty-four
hexagrams each of which form the subject of an essay
in the text of the Yi. The lines increase in an arith-
metical progression whose common difference is one
and the figures in a geometrical progression whose
common ratio is two.

The eight trigrams were called:—

"*Khien*, heaven, sky, celestial sphere.

*Tui*, watery exhalations, vapours, clouds.

*Li*, fire, heat, sun, light, lightning.

*Chen*, thunder.

*Sun*, wind, wood.

*Khan*, water, rivers, lakes, seas.

*Ken*, mountains.

*Khwun*, earth, terrestrial matter."[1]

*Khien* represented by three undivided strokes is
"Unalloyed Yang." Khwun represented by three divided strokes is "Unalloyed Yin." In the mixed
groups the lower line indicates the place of most
importance.

*Khien* symbolises Heaven which directs the great

[1] De Groot's *Religious System in China*.

beginnings of things, and *Khwun* the Earth which gives to them their completion.

*Khien* and *Khwun* are the gate of the Yi. Movement and rest are the regular and inherent qualities of each.

The six minor trigrams or children are water and fire, thunder and wind, mountains and large bodies of water.

In China the four "heaven spirits" were cloud, rain, wind, thunder, and the worship of mountains and rivers was closely associated with the worship of heaven.

The trigrams contain the three powers, heaven, earth and men. These three are one and the same. When doubled into hexagrams the three powers unite and are one. "But there are the changes and movements of their (several) ways and therefore there are separate places for Yin and Yang and reciprocal uses of the hard and soft."[1]

This system of divination was really an attempt—and an amazingly clever one at that—to explain the origin of nature on mathematical principles. Numbers were conceived of "not as relations predicable of things but as constituting the essence of things." Numbers were the rational reality to which appearances as recognised by the senses may be reduced. Troward

[1] Legge's trans., *Yi King*.

must have studied the Yi for he speaks of the "three great principles into which all forms of manifestation may be analysed—the Masculine, Positive or Gener-

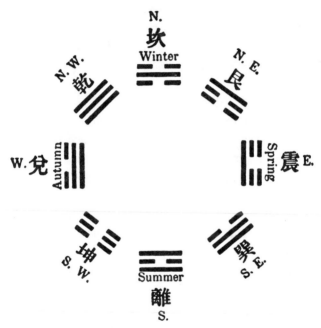

**ARRANGEMENT OF TRIGRAMS ACCORDING TO WEN WANG.**

ating Principle; the Feminine, Receptive or Formative Principle; and the Neuter or Mathematical Principle which, by determining the proportional relations between the other two, gives rise to the principles of variety and multiplicity." [1]

[1] *Bible Mystery and Bible Meaning*, p. 71, T. Troward.

In the Yi production and re-production are what is called change. The whole system, in fact, is based upon the "contractions and expandings, recedings and approachings of the productive and completing powers of the even and odd numbers."

*Yang* being represented by an undivided line or one stroke ――――― therefore all odd numbers belong to *Yang*.

*Yin* having a divided line or two strokes ―― ―― hence all even numbers belong to *Yin*.

Three was assigned to heaven and two to earth.

Heaven was high, earth low. That which is high is noble, honourable. Things low are mean.

*Yang* was nine, and *Yin* six.

*Nine* being the triple multiple of the undividable number which represents *Yang* or Heaven, means in Chinese the "fullness of Yang."

In Hebrew the number nine was equivalent to Truth. When multiplied the immutable number nine reproduces itself. Thus $2 \times 9 = 18$. $1 + 8 = 9$. $3 \times 9 = 27$. $2 + 7 = 9$ and so on.

In the minor trigrams those which contain only one undivided line belong to *Yang*. The *Yang* trigrams represent one ruler and two subjects thus indicating superiority. Those which contain two undivided lines belong to *Yin* and signify two rulers and one subject symbolising inferiority, weakness, dissension.

The system or philosophy as developed in the Yi King is strikingly unlike the majority of religious beliefs. There is no sort of a notion conveyed of the ultimate marriage of heaven and earth, nor of a day when the lion and the lamb are going to lie down together. On the contrary, the Chinese, who are intensely practical as well as mystical, seem to have accepted the fact that the lion and the lamb are temperamentally unfitted for any permanent association, and that heaven and earth can only unite for the purpose of production.

The changeableness of human affairs—union gives way to separation—from separation comes re-union —this is the theme of the Yi King. "The ever changing phenomena of nature and human experience."

"Sun goes, moon comes. Moon goes, sun comes. Cold goes, heat comes. Heat goes, cold comes. That which goes becomes less, that which comes increases. Thus the seasons, year, all life completes itself."

## VIII.—THE FOUR SUPERNATURAL
## CREATURES OF THE CHINESE

THE four supernatural, divinely constituted beasts
—the **Unicorn,** the **Phœnix,** the **Tortoise,** the **Dragon**
—are called the *Ling.* Couvrez translates this as
*"animaux qui donnent des présages."* Dr. de Visser
believes that it has a stronger meaning and translates
it as spiritual beings, and calls them the "four spiritual
animals, *par excellence."* The dragon being the
fullest of *Yang* is the chief and is constantly represented in Chinese art.

The **Dragon** has figured in the mythologies and
folk tales of nearly all ancient races as the personification of evil and chaos.

The Chinese and also the Japanese—who borrowed
so many of their religious ideas from the Chinese—
give a much wider meaning to the dragon.

It is almost impossible for the Western mind to
grasp the mystical subtleties that are embodied in
their dragon symbolism. The **Dragon** and all that it
implies enters into the very warp and woof of Chinese
thought and imagery.

It is the symbol of power, royalty, sovereignty. It
symbolises floods, clouds, rains. Water is a source of

greatest good as well as evil, and in China the dragon becomes the most potent symbol of the blessing, the rain giving gods of water. Above all else—that thought so dear to the Chinese mind, that sees the eternal in the fleeting—the dragon is the spirit of change. "Infinity is the Fleeting, the Fleeting is the Vanishing, the Vanishing is the Reverting."

The **Dragon** is called the "beloved symbol of the Taoists."[1]

"The Dragon can be bigger than big, smaller than small, higher than high, lower than low." He wields the power of transformation and invisibility. He conceals himself or becomes brilliant. When he breathes his breath changes to a cloud upon which he rides to heaven. He mounts to the sky at the time of the spring equinox. When he flies too high the "thirsty earth must wait for his blessings and sorrow prevails." At the time of the autumnal equinox he plunges down into the depths. He sleeps in the pools in winter and arouses himself in the spring. He is the god of thunder and appears in the rice fields as rain, or as dark clouds in the sky.

The symbol of imperial sovereignty is an ascending dragon which belches forth a ball. The ball in this case is the thunder and not the sun pursued by the dragon.

Sometimes the object depicted between **Two**

[1] Kakuzo's *The Book of Tea*, p. 50.

**Dragons** is shaped like a spiral, the spiral denoting the roll of thunder from which issues a flash of lightning.

The **Dragon** devours the moon during an eclipse, and the **Ball** between two dragons is sometimes the **Moon** which the dragons are attempting to swallow. The conjunction of moon and water was obviously a magical one, used to draw down the fertilising rains.

More frequently the ball is a "precious pearl," a form of the *tama* or sacred gem which typified the spirit or divine essence of the gods, and also the force which controls the ebb and flow of tides.

The **Pearl** was believed to be the "concrete essence of the moon distilled through the secret workings of the secondary principle of nature within the mussel of the shell which produces it. Hence it acts as a charm against *fire*, the active or primary principle."[1]

The intense desire of the dragons to regain possession of this jewel which has been wrested from them by the covetousness of man is a favourite subject in myth and legend, and constantly appears in Oriental art, where the dragons are depicted either guarding it or battling for it.

The dragons have been divided into five sorts, but the usual number in China, when used in an ethical or abstract sense, are four: The Celestial dragon who upholds the heavens, the Spiritual or Divine dragon

[1] Mayer's *Chinese Reader's Manual.*

of wind and rain, the Earth dragon of rivers and streams, and the Dragon of Hidden Treasure who watches over the wealth concealed from mortals.

The connection of **Dragons** with **Pearls** is here manifestly clear. The masters of the sea would jealously guard its treasures.

The **Dragon** diffused light. "A black dragon vomits light and makes Darkness (*Yin*) turn into Light (*Yang*)."

The **Dragon** in Japan is the symbol of the Mikado whose garments are the robes of the dragon, whose face is called the dragon face and who is seated on a dragon throne.

The dragon is depicted with flame-like wings or appendages curving out from shoulders and hips. Its feet are given three, four or five claws. The Japanese dragon has three claws. The imperial dragon of China is always given five. This may be because Japan has three kinds and China five, or possibly it symbolises the Chinese myth that the dragon in water covers himself with five colours.

De Groot places the azure dragon as highest in rank among all the dragons in China because blue is the colour of the East. According to other authorities the yellow dragon is the most honoured.

The **Blue Dragon** symbolises the vital spirit of water.

The **Yellow Dragon** is the essence of divine manifesting power.

As far back as 2700 B.C. Yao the dragon was one of the six symbolic figures painted on the upper garment of the emperor.

Imperial coffins used to be painted with a sun, moon, bird, tortoise, dragon and tiger. The burial garments for women had dragons embroidered on them surrounded by clouds, bats, phœnixes, stags, tortoises and cranes—emblems of fertilising rains, longevity, bliss, immortality, happiness.[1]

Someone has said that the dragon is to China what the Lion and the Unicorn are to England, and the Eagle to America. We may fairly infer, however, that it has a much higher spiritual meaning.

Dragon painting reached its zenith in the thirteenth century.

The **Unicorn,** *K'i-lin* in Chinese and *Ki-rin* in Japanese (*K'i* male, and *lin* or *rin* female), was supposed to combine both masculine and feminine principles, and has figured in all countries from prehistoric days as a symbol of purity, strength of body

[1] "To present an aged parent with one of these costly and splendid mantles, known as 'longevity garments' is esteemed by the Chinese an act of filial piety and a delicate mark of attention. As the garment purports to prolong the life of its owner, he often wears it, especially on festive occasions." Fraser's *The Golden Bough,* abridged edition, p. 36.

THE HORNED YELLOW DRAGON
(Henry Doré, S. J., *Researches into Chinese Superstition*.)

LOTUS FLOWER, STORK AND PHŒNIX

THE CHINESE UNICORN

THE PHŒNIX

(Henry Doré, S. J., *Researches into Chinese Superstition*)

and virtue of mind. Among the Chinese it was considered to be the incarnate essence of the five primordial elements and was believed to live one thousand years, only appearing when some great event is about to occur. It ranks first among the four sacred animals that preside over the destinies of China.

The **Unicorn** is found on the earliest examples of Chinese art, where it closely resembles the dragon-horse. It is depicted on ancient Egyptian hieroglyphics. It is spoken of in the psalms, "But my horn shalt thou exalt like the horn of the unicorn" (Ps. 92 : 10), also in other books of the Old Testament.

The **Unicorn** was adopted by the Christians as a symbol of female chastity in allusion to the fable that it "could never be captured except by a virgin stainless in mind and life." It was given only to the Virgin Mary[1] and St. Justina.

In the art of the Renaissance the **Unicorn** and the **Lion** are frequently depicted together.

The **Phœnix** (*Féng*), a fabulous bird of mystic nature, second among the supernatural creatures, is associated with the sacred *ho-o* or *ho-ho*, a huge eagle, represented

---

[1] "The unicorn is hunted by the archangel Gabriel and driven into the lap of the Virgin by which was understood the immaculate conception." Jung's *Psychology of the Unconscious*, Note **525.**

in the earliest art in China bearing off large animals
in its claws. It strongly resembles the sacred *garuda*
of the Hindus. Later the *ho-o* becomes a compound
of the peacock and the pheasant. The female was
called *hwang* or *luan* and this combined with *féng* the
male becomes *féng-hwang* or *féng-luan*, the name by
which this wondrous bird was usually designated,
indicating as in the case of the *k'i-lin* (the unicorn)
that it is supposed to unite in itself the two forces
masculine and feminine. It is not identified with the
phœnix of Egypt which burned itself and rose again
from its own ashes, and was such a potent symbol of
resurrection and immortality, although this, too, is
believed to be the essence of fire, and Chinese mystics
regarded it as typifying the entire world. "Its head
is heaven, its eyes the sun, its back the crescent
moon, its wings the wind, its feet the earth, its tail
the trees and plants."[1] Its plumage of five colours
symbolised the five cardinal virtues, and its appearance was the forecast of wise and beneficent rulers.

The **Phœnix** as a royal emblem was given to
the Empress, as the **Dragon** was the symbol of the
Emperor.

The **Tortoise** (*Kwei*). It was the "divine tortoise"
who presented to the sage Lü a scroll of writing on its
back made up of the numbers 1 to 9. Lü made this

[1] *Japanese Art Motives*, Maude Rex Allen.

the "basis of his nine-fold exposition of philosophy or nine divisions of the Great Plan."[1]

The **Tortoise** was believed to conceive by thought alone, it had the power of transformation, and would create by its breath clouds, fogs or palaces of enchantment. It was supposed to live one thousand years, but when represented in art with long bushy tail it indicates that it has attained its ten thousandth year.

The Chinese had two chief modes of divination, one by the stalks of the yarrow and the other by the tortoise shell. The latter was considered the nobler method, and thus the tortoise held the secrets of life and death.

The **Tortoise** is a symbol of longevity, also fecundity, and was used in the latter sense by the Egyptians. In Greek art Venus is sometimes represented standing on a tortoise.

The **Tortoise** besides having the power of divination, transformation, longevity and fecundity was

---

[1] "The five elements also figure prominently in 'The Great Plan' which is an ancient imperial manifesto on the art of good government. There it is stated that like everything else they are produced by the *yang* and the *yin*, being the natural results of that two-fold breath which will operate favourably or unfavourably upon the living or the dead, according to the combination in which they are mixed. All misfortunes are said to arise from a disturbance of the five elements in a given situation, and thus the Chinese are very careful not to interfere with nature." *Chinese Thought*, Paul Carus, p. 46.

said to carry the world on its back. The myth is almost universal. Sometimes it supports the treasure mountain of the mystic jewel, the *Tama* or Sacred Pearl. In Japan it upholds the mountain abode of the gods. In the Hindu legend the tortoise sustains an elephant upon whose back rests the world. The Delaware Indians believed that the Central World Tree grew out of the middle of the back of a tortoise. Among the Seneca's the sky mother fell into a great pit on the wings of a waterfall who placed her on a turtle's back. In an ancient Arab myth a whale performs the 'all sustaining office' of the tortoise. Earthquakes were caused by the awakening of the earth tortoise—the tortoise yawned and all nature was convulsed.

According to Jung the Indian symbolism of a world bearing animal, an elephant standing on a tortoise, is a part of the same symbolism. "The elephant has chiefly masculine phallic significance. The tortoise like every shell animal is feminine."[1]

And all this dovetails perfectly into the trailing history of the feminine principle, accused of being chaos, of giving birth to the world, of bestowing the apple of discord and of stirring up things generally whenever she ceases to be quiescent. She amuses, entertains, annoys, delights, destroys; is capable of

[1] Jung's *Psychology of the Unconscious.*

wild, unreasoned malevolence; has steadfast, patient endurance—and *carries the whole world on her back.*

A quaint way to tell us a deeply psychological truth, but the ancients delighted in quaint and fantastic ways of picturing the spirit and flow of life. Thus the tortoise sustaining an elephant, upon whose back rests the world, is simply another symbolic device to remind us of that immensely important pair who create, uphold, tear down.

The **Tortoise** as a support is a favourite subject in bronze.

## IX.—ANIMAL SYMBOLISM IN CHINESE ART

*"Exposer les animaux, c'était réellement passer en revue l'art Chinois entier."* [1]

THE BIRD OF FIRE.
Bayley, *Lost Language of Symbolism.*

CHINA has symbolised by animals the cosmological beliefs that for countless ages have impressed themselves upon her intellectual, moral and social life.

Her art has been called "symbolical narration."

This primitive symbolism which dominates Chinese art is based largely upon the zodiacal position of certain animals. Upon this juxtaposition has been woven an intricate network of fanciful ideas.

The four cardinal points and the four seasons were thus represented:

> East, Spring, Blue, Dragon,
> South, Summer, Red, Bird.
> West, Autumn, White, Tiger,
> North, Winter, Black, Tortoise.

[1] *Les Animaux dans l'Art Chinois*, H. d'Ardenne de Tizac.

In this way the east was the azure dragon, the south the vermilion bird, west the white tiger and north the sombre warrior.

The **Tortoise** belonging to the *Yin* principle was regarded as feminine, and Chinese legend associates it with the serpent in much the same way that the serpent is related to the feminine principle in nearly all primitive myths and legends. Associated thus the **Serpent** and **Tortoise** when depicted together are called the "Dark Warriors" and typify the north.

"Cloud follows the dragon, Wind follows the tiger." The symbolism of the **Dragon** and the **Tiger** is of great antiquity preceding that of *Yang* and *Yin* although the idea conveyed is the same. The **Dragon** typified heaven, the sky, fertility, the Tiger, chief of all land animals the earth. Their union expressed that belief so old and so persistently held that perfect bliss and happiness are only attained when the dualistic forces are in equilibrium. Without the earth heaven would have no way of expressing itself. The earth, unless revivified by heaven, would be only a cold, dark, inert mass, the region of death and decay.

The dragon and tiger also symbolised the two constellations Scorpio and Orion.

The **Bird** and **Tortoise,** emblems respectively of *Yang*, summer, and *Yin*, winter only appear after the dragon and tiger.

In the development of the *Yang* and *Yin* concept *Yang* the luminous principle typifies the south and noon, *Yin* cold, obscure, dark, typifies north and midnight. The morning corresponds to spring, the evening to autumn. The animals also respond to this classification. The *Yin* animals are those which seek damp, obscure places. They are of cold nature, patient, slow, often burrowing in the earth. The most typical are the ox, rat, pig, tortoise. The *Yang* animals are hot-blooded loving light,—such as the horse, goat, cock, quail (the latter is transformed into the pheasant and finally becomes the phœnix).

The **Twelve Animals** of the Chinese Zodiac are: the rat, ox, tiger, hare, dragon, serpent, horse, goat, monkey, cock, dog, pig.

These represent at once the twelve divisions of the zodiac, the twelve months and the twelve double hours of the day. Each one, presiding over a special hour of the day and night, is supposed to exert an influence which reflects its own peculiar characteristics.

"This zodiac corresponds to the 'Twelve Earthly Branches' which together with the 'Ten Heavenly Stems' form a series of sixty combinations used for naming the years, months, days and hours. Each year, month, day and hour, therefore, is associated with one of these twelve animals and every Chinese knows well under which animal he is born. It is essential that he should do so, for no important step throughout his life is undertaken unless under the auspices of his particular animal. Indeed, this mysterious influence extends even beyond his life and is taken into consideration in the disposal of his corpse." [1]

These twelve animals were also affiliated with the five elements, and as symbolic motifs were constantly made use of by the Chinese artist.

The **Crow** is a Chinese symbol of the sun, and according to tradition a three-legged crow lived in the sun. It is a favourite subject also in Japan, and is often painted with the sun as background. Among the twelve symbols of power given by Giles [2] (actual symbolism unknown) are the sun with a three-legged raven in it, and the moon with a hare in it pounding the drug of immortality.

Among the Chinese the moon represented the concrete essence of the feminine principle in nature and thus directed everything that belonged to the *yin* principle such as darkness, earth, water, etc. "The Vital essence of the Moon governs Water; and hence when the Moon is at its brightest the tides are high." Chinese and Indian legends agree in making the hare, frog and toad inhabitants of the moon.

[1] *Symbolism in Chinese Art*, W. Percival Yegg, p. 21.
[2] *History of Chinese Pictorial Art*, Herbert A. Giles.

Eight trees also were said to flourish in the moon. One, the cassia tree Wu Kang, the Man in the Moon was condemned to hew down. The trunk of the tree closed after each blow of the axe. The leaves of the cassia conferred immortality upon those who ate of them.

The association of **Moon** and **Hare** is a very old one, and has been attributed to the mysterious effect of the moon upon the hare. On clear moonlight nights the hare were wont to gather together in bands and indulge in weird play, silent and bizarre as if under the influence of some subtle and transforming elixir of life.

The **Cock** within a circle is a Chinese symbol of the Sun, and the Bird of Dawn is often depicted clapping wings of gold as the sun rises behind him. It is the bird of *Yang* and as the spirits of darkness belong to the *Yin* principle, the cock was used at funerals to dissipate the power of evil spirits. It was believed, too, that the spirits of darkness were put to flight each morning by the crowing of the cock. It is a prominent symbol of the Shinto religion and is shown standing on the temple drum which summons the faithful to prayers.

The **Cock** and **Dog** symbolise the opposites. The one, symbol of the east, *Yang*, who announces the rising of the God of Day, is opposed to the second who belongs to the *Yin* and the west and who takes up his responsibilities of guardianship as the night descends.

The **Pig** and **Serpent** are another of these *Yin* and *Yang* associations, which seems to be also founded on the well known fact that the hog is immune to the bite of serpents and does not hesitate to destroy them.

The **Fish** is an universal symbol of fertility.

**Two Fish** are a very common Chinese symbol of marriage and hence fecundity.

The **Unicorn with a Parrot** on its back, the former symbolised dumb justice, and the parrot, its talkative advocate.

The **Stag** is an emblem of old age, joy, monetary riches.   A **White Stag** is depicted with the god of longevity.

The **Elephant** among Buddhists typified care, caution and puissant dignity.  Buddha is said to have descended to earth in the form of a **White Elephant.** Thus the elephant is often depicted kneeling before the Sacred Bodhi Tree, or again Buddha as a child is represented on the back of an elephant who with its trunk, presents to him the sacred lotus flower.

The **White Horse** plays an important part in Chinese Buddhism.  It was on a white horse that Buddha left his palace to become an ascetic and a white horse saved him from the Râshasa or cannibal demons.

Buddha was supposed to have been born eleven

times as a deer and Buddha's Wheel of Law is frequently portrayed between **Two Deer** or **Two Gazelles.**

The **Lion** symbolised the Church Triumphant of Buddhism.

**Lions in Pairs**—called by the Japanese the Dogs of Foo (Foo meaning Buddha) are found before Buddhist Temples and doorways, palaces and tombs, and are nearly always placed east and west, the male lion typifying *Yang* and east, the female *Yin* and west. They have grotesque, grinning faces, the mouth of the female is closed, that of the male is open. Frequently one is blue and the other green. Their office is that of protectors, the almost universal symbolism of the lion.

**Tiger** and **Dragon** symbolise power.

The **Tiger** is depicted not only as a mount for the gods of exorcism and immortality, but as a creature of superhuman power,—demon dispelling and demon destroying—a prodigy of strength. The Taoist god of wealth rides on a tiger who guards the magic money chest. The god of riches is also shown with a tiger on one side and dragon on the other. It is the patron of gamblers, and images of it are found in gambling places, where it is represented holding money in its forepaws. Affixed to houses it was a charm against spectres and evil visitations.

The **Goose** is the "Bird of Heaven," a symbol of *Yang* the highest creative energy, of love, constancy, truth, inspiration. Thus a painting of wild geese flying low against a misty background, means to the beholder far more than the surface representation.

So, too, with the **Mandarin Duck** which symbolised connubial love and fidelity and depicted together are emblems of undying faithfulness.

The **Four Seasons** had each their flower. Summer has the lotus, Autumn the chrysanthemum, Winter the wild plum and Spring the tree peony. These, too, have their symbolic affiliations with bird and beast, and arranged in various groupings to express certain definite or mystical ideas, are called rebuses.

A feature of Chinese decoration from the earliest days, the majority of these symbolic motives are concerned with happiness attained by material prosperity and 'longevity.'

The **Five Blessings** are: longevity, riches, peacefulness and serenity, love of virtue, a happy death.

The **Five Eternal Ideals** are: humaneness, uprightness, propriety, insight, fidelity.

**Five Relations of Mankind**: That between emperor and subject, father and son, brother and brother, husband and wife, friend and friend.

The characters which stand for the "five blessings" and also the "five eternal ideals" are the most popular symbols in China, and of these the most used of all are the characters 'longevity' and 'blessing.' They appear on decanters, on the bottom of teacups, on buckles, pins, furniture, textiles and robes.

**Five Bats** symbolise the 'five blessings.'

The **Bat** alone is a symbol of happiness.

"Blessing is called *fu* in Chinese, which is the exact homophone of *fu* meaning bat, and so the five blessings *wu fu* are frequently represented by five bats."[1]

The popularity of the word "longevity" (*sheu* or *shou*) meaning years, a long and prosperous life, birthday, old age, to endure forever, and also suggesting immortality exceeds that of any other word, and the character is represented in innumerable ways.

Regarded as the highest blessing, the symbols and animals that typify 'longevity' are constantly appearing in Chinese art.

The **Peach Tree, Pine Tree, Tortoise, Crane, Stork, Dove, Stag, Bamboo** are all symbols of 'longevity' and appear singly or in various groupings.

The **Crane** ranks next in importance to the Phœnix, and was believed to transport to heaven those who had attained immortality. It is often represented standing on the back of a tortoise. Candlesticks are made in this form.

The **Stork** is one of the symbols of *hsiao* 'filial piety' which Confucius defined as "carrying on the aims of our forefathers" and is thus given to father and son in the Relations of Mankind. The wide-spread

[1] *Chinese Thought*, Paul Carus, p. 17.

legend of nursery days that storks bring babies is thought to have been derived from this association—"Doing as our fathers have done."

The **Pine Tree** alone is a puissant and highly reverenced symbol of 'longevity.' Frequently the god of longevity is depicted at the foot of a pine tree, with the Crane perching on a branch above. The god of long life is generally portrayed as an old man with long beard, his robes embroidered with the character *sheu* (long life). He is frequently given the peach of immortality and the Sacred Fungus and is associated with the stag and other symbols of 'longevity.'

The **Cicada** appears as an emblem of resurrection.

The **Praying Mantis** represents courage, persistence.

**Butterflies** are a favourite subject and typify love and felicity.

The **Bamboo,** which yields but never breaks, is a greatly loved symbol of constancy and 'longevity.'

The **Bamboo** and **Sparrow** symbolise friendship.

The **Bamboo** and **Crane** signify long life and happiness.

The **Tortoise** and **Peach** symbolise 'longevity' and immortality.

The **Lotus flower, Stork** and **Phœnix** typify numerous and happy descendants.

Certain birds are associated with certain flowers, and flowers and the months when they appear make them the logical associates of the zodiacal animals that preside over those months. The combinations are almost without end, more so, perhaps, because formed on so definite and interlocking a plan.

Space lacks to give more than a hint of a symbolism so vast and far reaching, based on a philosophy of life that makes everything in nature tributaries of *Yang* and *Yin*, and that to lovers of art and metaphysics opens up such fascinating vistas of speculative thought.

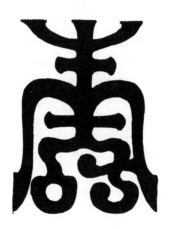

# X.—THE SUN

*Whoso venerates the Sun that is immortal, brilliant, swift horsed . . . he venerates Ormazd, he venerates the Archangels, he venerates his own soul.*—From the Nyaishes or Zoroastrian Litanies of the Sun.

BACK of their nature worship there seems to have been, from very early days, a belief in one great God who created the lesser gods, whom the ancients worshipped, not as the divine, self-created power, but as manifestations of that power which is "immutable, eternal, unfathomable, not to be fully known."

It is probable that the Sun worshippers placed this power in the sun as later cults have said God is in the heavens, making the sun, as the highest manifestation of creative energy and life, the abiding place of the mysterious, unknown *primum mobile*, and thus it came to typify the Supreme Creator, the source of all Life, Light, Power and was addressed as that power.

Worship of the sun-god Ra became first prominent in Egypt at Heliopolis and in the Fifth Dynasty (2700 B.C.) was adopted as the religion of the state. The Egyptian religion has been called a solar drama. It is the drama of Life and Death, of struggle between the power of Light and Life and the malignant power of Darkness. The mighty Sun, Lord of All Life spends his nights in mortal combat with his evil brother Set, now disguised as Apep, the huge serpent of mist and darkness. When the sun appears in the morning as the youthful Horus, ever gloriously young, there is rejoicing. Good has triumphed over evil. Yet the drama begins again as night falls—always the never ending contest, if Light and Life are to win over Darkness and Death. The same struggle is represented in other mythologies. Apollo slays the python. Zeus defeats the Titans. Thor fights with Sorcerers and giants and Indra with the dragon Vritra.

The return of the sun, too, featured immortality —the Sun that re-news itself. The sun-god as thus figured becomes the prototype of all heroes and dragon-slayers. He is a mighty warrior, young and of incredible beauty, the protector who struggles with sin and chaos, the Great Lover who rescues imprisoned damsels, who conquers demons and wicked tyrants, defeats darkness and death itself, emerging triumphant in the splendour of renewed life and power. He is the Prince Charming who releases the ice maiden. Siegfried, St. George, King Arthur—all the heroic dragon-slayers play the immortal part. Cinderella the little fire tender becomes the bride of the Prince of Light. Bluebeard slaying his seven wives is the sun slaying the dawn. Many of the fairy stories that go back to the dawn of human history and are found to be practically the same among widely scattered races, become clear and full of poetic beauty when interpreted as solar myths.

The **Sun** was the "great Proteus, the universal metamorphist."

MYCENÆAN VASE.
Old Salamis.
Evans, *Mycenæan Trees and Pillar Cult.*

Sun worship was of great antiquity in Babylonia, also in Assyria, Persia, Phœnicia, and Asia Minor. In India "Surya is the sun seen in the sky." Unlike the Chinese who make heaven the highest good, the Japanese place their highest deity in the sun and it is the sun-goddess Ama-terasu ("heaven shining great

deity") from whom the living emperor claims descent.
The Druids were sun worshippers as well as tree
worshippers.  Knossos on the island of Crete was the
seat of the great sun worship of the pre-historic
Greek civilisation, and  the legend of the Minotaur is
supposed to be the mythical marriage of the sun and
moon.

The **Sacred Double Axe** as a religious symbol of
the sun is pre-eminently associated with the island of
Crete.

The **Axe** among the Egyptians was also a symbol
of the sun, and called the "Clever one," the "Cleaver
of the way." and belongs to the same class of symbols
as the hammer, sword, cross.  Why marking a track
through a forest with an axe is still spoken of as
"blazing a trail," is an interesting speculation on the
persistence of ancient customs and ideas.


The Egyptian hieroglyph of the sun-god Ra was
a point within a circle.  The life of Indian and
Egyptian gods was in the egg.  The "dot within the
circle," a symbol that goes back to remotest times
may have typified the seed within the egg.  This is
the Orphic egg, symbol of the universe whose yolk in
the middle of a liquid surrounded by an encompassing
vault, represented the globe of the sun floating in
ether, and surrounded by the vault of heaven.

A **Point** within a **Circle** is still used as the astronomical sign of the sun. In Egypt the **Circle** also symbolised the course of the sun about the universe.

The **Sun** was likened to a hawk or falcon taking his lofty flight across the sky, and from this may have originated the Egyptian symbol of the deity, a **Sun-Disk with the Outspread Wings of a Hawk.** This solar emblem of life, omnipotence, majesty was also widely venerated in Asia Minor. The Assyrians introduce a warrior with bow and arrow in the winged sun-disk.

The **Arrow,** symbol of fertility, rain, lightning, war, famine, disease, death is associated with the sun,

moon and atmospheric gods. Apollo gave Hercules a solar arrow. Apollo's arrows are the sun's rays.

The **Rays of the Sun** were also called the hair of the sun-god. The strength of the sun departs when he is shorn of his hair in winter. Hair was sacred to the sun-god, cutting the hair a sacrificial offering. The

priest's tonsure represents the disk of the sun. The
Arabs shaved their heads in imitation of the sun. The
priests of Egypt and India had shaven heads. Hair
as a source of strength in the story of Samson and
Delilah has led scholars to interpret this as a solar
myth.

**Crowns** worn by kings and emperors symbolised
the sun's rays.

The Egyptian **Cartouche** or oval in which the name
of a royal person was enclosed, was originally a circle
symbolising the course of the sun around the universe.
Thus the king's name inside a circle denoted his
association with the sun-god, that his power followed
the course of the sun, and that he and those of his
name, like the sun, would endure forever.

The **Nimbus, Aureole or Glory** used in Christian
art to distinguish holy personages is derived from
the solar disk, which in ancient art was given to
royal persons to express their divine origin and their
association with the might and power of the Supreme
and All Creative Sun.

**Amber** because of its golden transparency was a
symbol of the sun and is still worn as an amulet
against evil and disease.

The **Lotus** is the symbol *par excellence* of the sun.

The **Scarabæus** or Sacred Beetle symbolised divine,
self-created power. The early Egyptians believed that
it had no female but deposited its generative seed in

round pellets of earth which it rolled about, thrusting
backward by means of the hind-legs, thus imitating
the sun which moving "from west to east turns the
heaven in the opposite way." Thus the beetle was
born anew from the egg which it alone had created,

HAWK ON LOTUS ANTHEMION.
Greek pottery fragment.
Goodyear, *Grammar of the Lotus.*

and was so highly reverenced by the Egyptians as a
symbol of self-existent being, that the wings of the
winged sun disk have been interpreted by some as
being those of the Scarabæus instead of the hawk.

The Chinese regarded the sun as the concrete
essence of the masculine principle and the source of
all light.

In Japan the temple of Isé is the shrine of the sun-
goddess and a metallic **Mirror,** emblem of the sun,
and a **Sword** and **Jewel** were handed on by the sun-
goddess to her grandson when he descended upon the

islands.   The **Sword** is the attribute of the storm-
god who is supposed to have taken it from a dragon's
tail, and whose descendants were rulers of Japan before
the descent of Ninigi the grandson of the sun-
goddess.[1]   The **Jewel** may be the **Cintamani,** the
magic gem which satisfies all desires.

The **Mirror** is the sole symbol in Shinto shrines.
The Egyptians, too, had the **Ank,** or **Sacred Mirror**
wherein every great deity contemplates perpetually
his own image.

"As in Aquinas the universe exists in a two-fold
manner, first ideally in the mind of God, and secondly
materially, externally to him, so that in Creation the
Almighty contemplates his own mind as in a
mirror."[2]


**Fire** played a large part in the ritual and ceremonies
of the sun worshippers.   The triangle, the universal
symbol of fire, was the primary form of the pyramid.
The **Pyramids** with their triangular sides were univer-

---

[1] "Every family in Japan claims descent from the gods who
followed the grandson of the Sun-Goddess in his descent upon the
island by the eight-rayed pathway of the clouds, thus intensi-
fying the national spirit which clusters round the unity of the
Imperial throne.   We always say 'We come of Ama' but whether
we mean the sky, or the sea, or the Land of Rama (?) there is
nothing, save the simple old rites of the Tree, the Mirror, and
the Sword, to tell."   *The Ideals of the East*, Kakasu Okakura,
pp. 15–16.

[2] *The House of the Hidden Places*, W. Marsham Adams.

sally recognised, not alone as tombs for the dead, but as monuments to the Light that is Eternal.[1]

**Altars** were frequently placed on the top of pyramids and upon these a fire was kept constantly burning.

**Fire** as a manifestation of heat and warmth on earth was worshipped as a secondary principle of solar creation. The belief that the sun died in winter only to be born again in the spring led to the feeling that man could and should aid the god of Light in his struggle with the opposing principle of Death. Thus as the forces of the Sun began to wane at midsummer, great bon-fires were lit to strengthen him. These fire festivals prevailed all over Europe down to the beginning of the nineteenth century, and are still observed in Norway, Bohemia and Brittany.[2]

Even after our era the cult of Mithraism or sun worship vied with Christianity in popular favour. In the fourth century Julian the Apostate, the last pagan to occupy the throne of the Cæsars attempted to revive sun worship, but the growing power of the Christian religion had become too strong to be set

[1] "Temples and monuments in pyramidal form are found accurately oriented in India, China, America, Java and the Polynesian Islands. That they symbolised the *Sun* and were something beyond Tombs may be inferred from the fact that within Egyptian Tombs small pyramids have been found bearing inscribed adorations of the Sun." Bayley's *Lost Language of Symbolism*.

[2] See *Life Symbols*, pp. 186–93.

aside. "The Invincible Sun, conquered at last, passed on its sceptre to the new religion of Life."

It was not until sometime between 354 and 360 A.D. that the Church adopted the 25th of December (the birthday of Mithra and other twice-born gods) as the date of the Nativity of Christ, the new sun of Righteousness in whom mankind saw again embodied the age-old, mystical idea of "Dying to Live."

Solar birds, solar animals, the swastika and solar wheel, all attributes of the sun are given under their own headings.

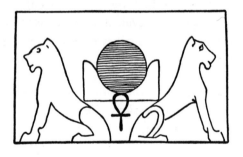

## XI.—THE MOON

*"Tanuanpat or Summer, the moon-god, the impulse which gives life to the three heavens, earth, air and sky, is called the 'rippling one who flies through the wide heavens wetting his horns'."*—Hewitt.

**LOTUS AND THE MOON-GOD.**

Assyrian seal.

Goodyear, *Grammar of the Lotus.*

Moon worship is believed by many scholars to be of even greater antiquity than sun worship. In the early days the **Moon** was regarded as masculine and the Sun was originally feminine.[1]

Sin, the moon-god of the Assyrians, is the god of wisdom. Thoth, the Egyptian god of learning, is a moon-god. Tanuanpat, the moon-god of ancient India, was called self-created, "the heavenly fire, offspring of himself." The moon-god as typifying summer was the uniting bond between spring the time of inception, and autumn the time of garnering. The harvest moon is the moon which ripens.

[1] "In ancient Babylonia where the population was essentially agricultural, the moon-god took precedence of the sun-god and was indeed reckoned his father." Frazer's *Adonis, Attis, Osiris,* p. 367.

The Egyptians, according to Plutarch, called the
moon the mother of the world and believed her to
have both the male and female nature "because she is
first filled and impregnated by the sun and then herself sends forth generative principles into the air, and
from thence scatters them down upon the earth."

There is a close connection between moon worship,
earth worship and water worship—all three representing the feminine or passive principle in nature. The
light of the moon on growing crops was believed to
be more beneficial than the scorching rays of the sun.

The **Moon** was thought to be the source of all
moisture. Everything from the sap of plants to the
blood of all beings was vitalised by the water of life
which the moon controlled.

The worshippers of Ea, the Sumerian god of water,
earth and heaven, believed that the essence of life was
to be found in the liquid element. Blood was the
vehicle of life and the worship of rivers and wells was
connected with a widespread belief that the blood of a
god flowed in the sacred waters. Sap was spoken of
in India as the "blood of trees."

The idea prevailed that no remission of sins was
possible without shedding of blood. It was also a
cardinal belief from remotest times that inspiration,
a fresh access of life, was derived from drinking blood.
The sacrament of eating bread and drinking wine
(partaking of the body and blood of the gods of

productivity) was a part of the ancient mysteries. And the idea of sanctifying one's self by assimilating a divine being goes back to remotest times. It was but a step up to transform the symbol into the Christian sacrament of the Eucharist. "He that . . . drinketh my blood, dwelleth in me and I in him" perpetuates an old belief founded on nature worship or the worship of life.

In the vibration of religious thought which gave supremacy first to the moon and then to the sun we may suppose that "even among the water worshippers of Eridu" the belief finally obtained that the sun and moon had a common origin as reflections of the One Supreme Absolute, the sun representing the generating, life giving power of the deity, the active principle, and the moon the passive principle. Thus the Egyptians recognised as their greatest gods the Sun and Moon (Osiris and Isis) and that the reciprocal action of the two great luminaries produced all life and growth upon the earth. It was the Sun the great Fecundator who communicated to the Moon the principles of generation which she afterwards disseminated through the air and the elements, which in turn transmitted them to the earth.

A **Sun-disk resting in a Crescent** symbolised the "conjunction of the divine pair."

The **Moon** symbolises the Celestial Mother. The

**Crescent Moon** is a symbol of virginity and is given to the "chaste Diana," and in Christian art to the Virgin Mary.

The **Moon** was called the "Awakener and Assembler of the stars," and a moon attended by stars is still perpetuated in the arms of Turkey and Egypt.

Under the influence of the lunar cult **Horns** became a symbol of divinity.

The **Crescent** is called the horned moon. In the illustration of two lions supporting the solar disk, the disk rests upon the conventionalised sacred horns of the moon crescent.

The Egyptian god Horus as the renewed sun bears on his head the tapering horns of the crescent upon which rests the solar disk.

Later the symbolism becomes realistic and horns of animals were used. Horns of the bull or cow typified honour, power. Those of the ram or goat signified fecundity.

The **Horns of Consecration** are prominent in the early Minoan worship. A. J. Evans considers that these suggest the horns of the altar of the Hebrew ritual, and may relate to the sacrificial oxen whose horns were set upon the altar as a part of primitive worship, "but it is more likely to have been derived from Egypt and to represent the lunar cult—the horns of the crescent moon."[1]

[1] *Mycenæan Trees and Pillar Cult*, A. J. Evans.

ARTEMIS (DIANA)
(Vatican, Rome.)

POSEIDON (NEPTUNE)
(Lateran, Rome.)

**Horns** also typified the sun's rays and were given also a phallic meaning. Everywhere they expressed power, light, strength and were used by the ancients as the crest and panache of heraldry were used, as a symbol of royal dignity.

**Horns** in all ages symbolised good luck and were placed in tombs and over doorways of houses as protective amulets to ward off evil influences.

The **Moon** was believed to have a mysterious and occult influence over the destinies of mankind. Our word lunacy is derived from *luna* the moon. To see the new moon over the right shoulder was a sign of good luck.

The **Cornucopia or Horn of Plenty** in which are displayed fruit and flowers is associated in Greek art with the great nature goddesses and gods of vegetation and the vintage.

Alone or in connection with its opposite the upright or straight line, the Crescent has lent itself to innumerable forms of ornamentation.

# XII.—THE WHEEL

*"A constantly moving something circling about a pure central point."*—Goethe.

THE **Wheel** with its spokes of which "none is the last" is one of the oldest symbols of the mystic power of the sun.

It is traced back to the sun disk crossed by the four cardinal points.

It is related that "Buddha at his birth took seven steps towards each of the four cardinal points, thus indicating the conquering of the circle or universe."

The **Wheel** is associated with the lotus flower, the symbol of the solar matrix.

The lotus flower with its centre surrounded by eight petals becomes the eight-spoked wheel of Buddhism. The eight spokes, or multiples of eight, symbolise the eight-fold path of self conquest.

The **Wheel** with the Buddhists is the Excellent Wheel of Good Law "which turns twelve times or three revolutions for each of the four noble truths."

Buddha is the wheel king, the 'king whose wheel rolls over the whole world.'

The turning of the wheel symbolised the doctrine of perpetual cycles of existence.

The **Wheel** in India in the days of the Veda typified the occult power of the sun.   It represented unending, perfect completion.

One of the symbols of Vishnu, who in later times superseded Varuna, the greatest god of the Rig-veda, is the discus or fiery wheel which "revolves and returns to the thrower like lightning."

**Karma** was called the 'wheel of fate that revolves relentlessly and unceasingly.'

"ROUE DE LA LOI."
Gaillard, *Croix et Swastika en Chine.*

The **Sun with Rays** becomes the 'thousand spoked wheel of victory.'

The **Solar Wheel** among the Assyrians was a symbol of life, and the god within the wheel not only was a god of war but of fertility.   The spirit of Ashur their great sun-god was thought to animate the wheel that brought the changing seasons.

Shamash the solar god of the Babylonians is shown seated on his throne with a sun-wheel in front of him. The spokes of the wheel are shaped like stars with three-fold rippling water rays.

The Vision of Ezekiel (Ez. 10), so frequently quoted, testifies to the prevalence and importance of the wheel symbol, and we may fairly infer that Ezekiel was making use of Assyrian symbolism which he had seen again and again when the Jews were in captivity.

In the fire festivals in honour of the sun, a lighted wheel was sent rolling down a hill.

The **Catherine Wheels** of modern fireworks, the *Wheel of St. Catherine* and the fiery disks of the ancients are presumably all derived from the solar wheel.

"ROUE DE LA LOI."
Gaillard, *Croix et Swastika en Chine.*

## XIII.—THE SWASTIKA

THE **Swastika** is a Sanskrit word composed of *su* good and *asti* being, with the suffix *ka*, and is the equivalent of "It is well," or "So be it."

It was reverenced in India three thousand years before the Christian era, and is stamped on archaic vases and pottery found in India, Persia, China, Italy, Greece, Cyprus; on ancient bronze ornaments in England, France, Etruria; on weapons and various ornaments in Germany and Scandinavia; on Celtic crosses in Ireland and Scotland; and in prehistoric burial grounds in Scandinavia, Mexico, Peru, Yucatan, Paraguay and the United States.

Apparently it was never adopted by the Phœnicians, Babylonians, Assyrians or Egyptians, although it has been found in Egypt, the inference being that it was brought there by the Greeks.

It was used before the Aryans commenced their migrations, and has been called the oldest Aryan symbol.

Wilson, the great authority on the swastika says: "Of the many forms of the cross, the swastika is the most ancient. Despite the theories and speculations of students its origin is unknown. It began before history and is properly classed as prehistoric."[1]

The **Swastika** has been given as an emblem to sun-gods, sky-gods, rain-gods; it has been called the monogram of Vishnu and Siva; it is the sun chariot of Agni; it is found in the footprints of Buddha; is the

NANDYAVARTA.
A third sign of the footprint of Buddha.

especial symbol of the esoteric doctrine of Buddha; Buddha is sometimes depicted in the 'swastika posture'—with legs crossed and arms cross-wise over chest; in Japan it symbolises Buddha's heart, and is frequently displayed on his breast. It has been given a phallic meaning. Others interpret it as typifying the generative or feminine principle from its appearance on statues of various nature goddesses—Ceres, Astarte, Hera and notably upon a leaden statuette of Artemis Nana of Chaldea found at Troy, where the swastika is shown on a triangular shaped shield.

[1] *The Swastika*, Thomas Wilson.

The **Swastika** is persistently associated with the *sacred fire-sticks*. Agni was the god of the fire-stick (swastika).

In Great Britain it was called *fylfot* from the Anglo-Saxon *fower-fot*—four footed or many footed.

The Druids were said to have shaped their trees in the form of the swastika or fylfot cross.

The **Swastika** was the cross of the Manicheans and was their sole symbol. During the second and third centuries the swastika was the only form of cross used by the Christians.

The swastika touched everywhere, and wherever it appeared, like the wheel, it was looked upon as the symbolical representation of solar energy. The swastika with its 'bent arms poised for flight' was the symbol of motion, good fortune, long life, and has been looked upon from earliest times as a charm or amulet that brings good luck.

John Newton gives an explanation of its origin which sounds reasonable enough. "Starting with the sun's disk as a circle, and wishing to represent its motion, sometimes they gave it wings, again they depicted it as a wheel, while motion in one direction was indicated by taking away part of the rim of the wheel leaving only sufficient to show its course. Thus came the swastika of the Hindus and the fylfot of the Northern races, one of the most universally diffused of all the mystic emblems of sun worship."[1]

Another of these whirling symbols of the sun is the **Triskelion** which proceeds apparently from the same

SICILIAN COIN.
Waring, *Ceramic Art in Remote Ages.*

symbolic idea as the swastika, its branches usually curved, radiating from a centre on a solar face. Found on ancient Greek shields and Roman coins, its rays sometimes take the form of legs, thus indicating conclusively the idea of motion, energy, victory. It has many variants, sometimes two, three or four arms or rays proceed from a central hub.

[1] *Origin of Triads and Trinities*, John Newton.

The well known **Trinity of Legs** with bent **knees**
has been used from the most ancient times **as the**
arms of Sicily and the Isle of Man.

From the swastika have been developed some **of**
the most exquisite running and interlacing designs.
One finds it on old bits of pottery, on rugs, fabrics
cunningly woven into labyrinthine forms that are
without beginning or end.  In Italy these were called
"Solomon's Knots" and were supposed to typify
divine inscrutability.

# XIV.—THE TRISULA

*"The plasticity of the Trisula is only equalled by its powers of absorption. It borrows from the vegetable kingdom as well as from man and the moon and the sun or flames."*—D'Alviella.

THE MONOGRAM OF BUDDHA.

The **Trisula** has been called a form of the thunderbolt, of the trident, of the Sacred Tree, a conventionalised form of the *fleur de lys*, a combination of sun disk and crescent, a form of the flame symbol,[1] and the caduceus of India. However widely scholars may differ as to their interpretation, all agree that it is universal, that it is one of the most important symbols of the ancient world, and so old that its origin is lost in the mists of a dateless antiquity.

As the *vajra*—"diamond or that which is indestructible" (usually translated thunderbolt)—the

[1] "If the moon crescent which arose above the lotus flower is represented with the flame symbol in the centre instead of the image, it forms a trident." A. Getty, *The Gods of Northern Buddhism.*

**Trisula** becomes the 'sceptre of diamonds' of Indra the storm god. The *vajra* or thunderbolt has been likened to the discus of Vishnu and like the celestial two headed mallet or double hammer of Thor, is a weapon of the gods typifying lightning, rain and thus life and fertility.

The Chaldeans figured a thunderbolt by a trident. In Nimroud it is held in the left hand of a god who holds an axe in the right. As the axe is a sun symbol and the trident is given to gods of storm and water we have here again the powerful union of fire and water. The *Vajra* appears in Mesopotamia as a double trident. Marduk in fighting with the monster Tiamat is depicted with a double trident in each hand. A trisula or trident with zigzag shaped points to typify lightning is frequently shown in the hands of Assyrian gods.

The **Trident** is the symbol of Poseidon (Neptune) the god of water, and the suggestion has been made that it typifies the third place the sea holds after heaven and air.

In Egypt the **Trident** or **Trisula** is associated with the winged sun disk.

The **Trisula** is one of the principal symbols of Siva who is usually represented holding a sceptre surmounted by a trisula. It is also given a high place

in the worship of Vishnu and signified male and
female or Rama and Sita. It was depicted as white
with the middle line red.

The thunderbolts given to Zeus with forked lightning projecting from either side bear a strong resemblance to the trisula.

In Buddhism the **Trisula** is given a prominent place
with the Stupa, the Sacred Tree, the Swastika and
the Excellent Wheel of Good Law. It is called "The
invocation of the highest," and when placed upon a
pillar surmounted by flames is the monogram of
Buddha. It is also one of the emblems of the Tri-
ratna.

At Carthage it was nearly always associated with
the Sacred Cone. Elsewhere it has been likened to
the *lingam* between two serpents. It has been con-
jectured that the curved lines were derived from
the Egyptian uræus. D'Alviella considers that the
Thunderbolt and Trisula are both derived from the
Trident (or three forces).

The **Sacred Trident** among the ancients symbolised
the heavenly triad.


Simpson gives an interesting interpretation that
seems more tenable than some others. "That the
Trisula is a development of solar and lunar forms as
symbols of creative power, would explain its universal
application. A symbol of like form, the Eî of Delphi, as

a monogram or letter had a high significance; a similar
form was a pronounced feature of sceptres in the hands

**FOOTPRINT OF BUDDHA AS CARVED ON THE AMARAVÂTI TOPE.**
From Schliemann's *Ilios*.

of gods, priests and kings, and whenever it appears it
typified the highest of the divine attributes. Even in
Plutarch's day the symbol was so old that its meaning was lost. . . . Some writers have identified the

Eî with the Hebrew EI (pronounced Jah), a form of the word Jehovah the root of which is 'to be,' 'to live.' . . . The explanation of Plutarch's, giving the symbol the idea of Being—of typifying that which is permanent and immutable as opposed to the constant change and variableness of nature gives it a sense very close to the majestic 'I am that I am' of the Pentateuch and gives it its exalted rank among symbols."[1]

Simpson goes on to say: "Viswakarma like the Greek Hephæstos the architect or artificer of the gods was said to have formed the discus of Vishnu, the trisula of Siva and the *vajra* or thunderbolt of Indra, making them from parings of Surya the sun which he put in a lathe and turned. Here we get the solar origin. . . . The most plausible theory which explains its sacred character is that it grew out of a combination of solar and lunar symbols. As these two symbols represent the dual creative or re-creative power of the universe, the power which continues all life—both animal and vegetable—their conjunction became a fit emblem of the divine energy which preserves and rules. It expressed the power which produced the cosmos out of chaos. . . . Symbolising the great mystery of life either in its inception or its continuance, it would equally symbolise the mystery of the future life. Thus it became a sceptre in

[1] *The Trisula Symbol*, William Simpson.

the hands of the gods representing their highest attribute."

He speaks as others have done of the central part of the trident being a development from the sun disk resting in the lunar crescent. The Assyrians also placed the disk of their sun-god in the crescent, thus representing the old androgynous conception of the deity which was prevalent in various parts of the ancient world, and was simply a way of personifying creative power.

In its sceptre form the **Trisula** has been associated with the pillar with a globular break in the middle and two uræus serpents curving up on either side. This symbol is often given to the Babylonian Ishtar.

1. EGYPTIAN URÆUS PILLAR. 2 and 3. CYPRO-MYCENÆAN COMPARISONS. 4. DUAL URÆUS STAFF OF ISHTAR.
Evans, *Mycenæan Trees and Pillar Cult.*

Sometimes the pillar with a break is a double cone, but the meaning is the same, typifying the dual cult which in the primal principle was believed to be androgynous and thus conforming in this symbology of the divided sceptre to the ancient Semitic conception of a bi-sexual godhead.

Like the lotus and swastika the trisula is used
decoratively, and was also looked upon as an amulet
or charm.

FRAGMENT OF STONE SLAB FROM THE ANCIENT MAYA CITY
OF MAYAPAN.

Ogee Swastika (Tetraskelion).

Wilson, *The Swastika.*

# XV.—SACRED BIRDS

*"The bird in which the breath and spirit is more full than in any other creature and the earth power least."*

—Ruskin.

PERSIAN
SEAL.

D'Alviella,
*Migration of
Symbols.*

THE **Bird** symbolised the spirit of the air, the spirit of life.

**Wings of a Bird** typified the wind.

**A Circle or Globe** with wings on either side was an Egyptian and Assyrian symbol of the deity.

In one of the early Egyptian triads of gods, Nut is heaven, Seb the earth and Shu the air or space which separates them. The hieroglyph of Shu is an ostrich feather, the least ponderable for its size, hence the symbol of space.

Maat the Egyptian goddess of truth carried a feather and in the judgment scene the heart of the deceased was weighed against a feather, the symbol of truth. Hence the saying "Heart as light as a feather."

The soul, which was commonly believed to be exhaled from the mouths of the dying in the last breath, was frequently pictured as a bird. It was a

part of the funeral rites of a Roman emperor to burn
his waxen image on a pyre. As the flames ascended
an eagle was let loose, symbolising the flight of the
soul to heaven.

DETAIL OF ASSYRIAN RELIEF, LAYARD.

In Egypt the soul is often portrayed as a human
headed bird hovering about the mummy. Or it is
depicted perched on a tree near by regarding curiously
its own funeral.

**The Hawk or Falcon, Vulture, Phœnix and Eagle** are birds of the sun, fire, wind, storms, immortality.

The **Hawk** because of the swiftness of its flight and because it was believed to be capable of outstaring the sun was given to all solar gods, and was particularly venerated in Egypt. Sometimes the head of a hawk is given to the body of a lion, the latter is also associated with the power and might of the sun.

The **Vulture** among the Egyptians, where decomposition sets in so rapidly, was regarded as an emblem of purification, of compassion, as a worker of all good. It also symbolised maternity, and the great mother goddesses are frequently represented as vultures, or wearing a headdress in the shape of a vulture.

The **Phœnix**, a fabulous bird of the sun has symbolised life and immortality from remotest antiquity. According to the legend it lives five hundred years or little more, when it will become young again and leave its old age. When this time arrives it makes for itself in some secret place in Arabia a nest of rarest spices. These, ignited by the heat of the sun, and fanned by the wings of the bird burst into flames consuming the phœnix, which arises from its own ashes, buoyantly young, to pursue "the same never ending life and re-birth."

In the Egyptian religion the phœnix was the embodiment of the sun-god Ra. Among the Romans where cremation was practiced, the phœnix was an emblem of resurrection and immortality. The Christians took it over from the pagans, using it as a symbol of immortality, and it was also used by the alchemists.

The **Eagle** is the symbol of royalty, power, authority, victory. Among the Greeks it symbolised supreme spiritual energy. Zeus is attended by an eagle. As a solar bird it is given to Ashur, the Assyrian sun-god and in the mythologies of Sumeria and Assyria the eagle is a symbol of fertility, of storm and lightning, the bringer of children and the deity who carries souls to Hades.

The **Eagle** is the antithesis of the serpent. Thus the contest between the sun and the clouds was often symbolised as a battle between eagles and serpents.

In its cruel aspect the **Eagle** is identified with the **Zu Bird,** a storm demon, a worker of disaster and evil. The Zu Bird symbolised also a phase of the sun, also fertility and slays serpents.

The **Garuda**—half eagle and half giant—is the solar vehicle of the Indian god Vishnu; is also called the "steed-necked incarnation of Vishnu." The Garuda is also identified with Agni, Brahma, Indra and Yama, the god of the dead.

The **Double-headed Eagle**—a form of the Garuda bird was worshipped by the Hittites as a symbol of omniscience. The Cherubim guarding the Tree of

Life are supposed to be modelled on the Double-headed Eagle. This Eagle of the Hittites figured until recent days on the royal arms of Austro-Hungary and Russia.

**EAGLE-HEADED FIGURES HOLDING SYMBOLIC CONE.**
Lajard, *Culte de Mithra.*

In Layard's *Nineveh* we read of the eagle-headed human figures depicted in colossal proportions on walls, or guarding the portals of chambers. These are sometimes contending with other mythic animals

**PERSIAN CYLINDER.**

such as a human-headed lion or bull. The fact that the eagle-headed figure was always victorious was interpreted by Layard as indicating the superiority of the intellect over mere physical strength.

Assyrian **Eagle-headed Genii** are depicted advancing towards the Sacred Tree holding the symbolic cone.

In Christian art St. John the Divine is given the eagle or again, when the four evangelists are represented as the four creatures of Ezekiel—a man, an ox, a lion, an eagle—he is sometimes depicted as an eagle.

The "primeval goose" that laid the golden egg of the world has come down through the ages as an object of endearing worship.

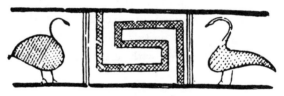

MEANDER DETAIL WITH SOLAR GEESE.
Greek "geometric" vase in the Louvre.

The **Goose** from earliest days, perhaps because of its sibillant hiss became associated with the sound of the rushing wind. The Hindus depict Brahma the Creator, the Breath of Life riding on a goose. The goose or 'breath bird' was sacred to Juno, the Queen of Heaven. In Egypt it was the attribute of Seb who in the creation myth is the 'chaos gander.'

In India, Egypt, Greece and Britain the goose is

associated with the sun and as a solar bird was given
to Osiris, Horus, Isis.  It was also sacred to Apollo,
Dionysos, Hermes, the Roman Mars, and Eros, the
god of love is depicted riding on a goose.  The oath
taken by Socrates and his disciples was "by the goose."

The **Goose** represented love and watchfulness.  It
was called the 'blessed fowl.'  The mystics likened
themselves to "unslumbering geese."  A goose with
flames issuing from its mouth typified the Holy Spirit
and symbolised the way of life and regeneration.

The **Goose** or Bird of Heaven was, as we have seen,
held sacred in China, also the crane, stork, and
mandarin duck.

COCK AND LOTUS.
From Goodyear's *Grammar of the Lotus.*

The **Cock,** the Bird of Fame is the acknowledged
emblem of the sun, and was sacred to Mithra, Zas
and nearly all the solar gods of antiquity.  It was
placed on church spires as an emblem of watchfulness.
This is probably the cock of St. Peter.  On the tops
of towers it becomes a *weathercock* which turns with
the wind.

The **Ibis,** a bird with legs like a crane, hooked beak and black in colour was associated with the moon and Thoth and deeply venerated by the Egyptians. It typified aspiration and perseverance was a symbol of morning and a destroyer of serpents.

The **Owl** was sacred to Athene (Minerva) goddess of wisdom. Owl-headed vases with breasts and the vulva represented by a large circle, the circle sometimes ornamented by an incised cross, were unearthed by Schliemann. These sacred vases were associated with the archaic Greek worship of Athene. Some were found with wings showing their sacred character.

The **Peacock** is sacred to Hera (Juno). In early Christian art it symbolised the resurrection.

**Doves** played a prominent part in the worship of Astarte, the Phœnician nature goddess. They were also attributes of Ishtar. The dove was a symbol of Bacchus the First Begotten of Love. Venus in Cyprus was known as "my lady of Trees and Doves." Doves bring ambrosia to Zeus. Doves and snakes were associated with the mother goddess of Crete, typifying her connection with air and earth. Doves were sacrificed to Adonis. In Vedic literature Yama is the god of the dead and his messengers are the owl and the pigeon. Doves and pigeons were sacred birds in Egypt.

A **Dove with an Olive Branch** was used as a symbol of Athene or renewed life.

In the Hebrew version of the flood Noah sends first a raven, then a dove and the dove returns the second time with an olive leaf in its mouth.

**Sacred Doves** are usually associated with the sepulchral cult. The "dove shrines" of Mycenæa are also connected with sacred trees and pillars.

In Christian art the **Dove** is the symbol of the Holy Ghost. It is pre-eminently the emblem of the soul and is thus seen issuing from the lips of dying martyrs. Symbolising the Holy Spirit it hovers about the Virgin and was also given to certain saints who were believed to be divinely inspired.

The **Woodpecker** was sacred among the Latins. A woodpecker as well as a wolf was said to have fed the twins Romulus and Remus.

**Crows in Pairs** were a symbol of conjugal fidelity in Egypt, where the same quality was given to them that attaches itself to the mandarin duck in China and the pigeon in other countries—that if either dies the other never consoles itself—never re-mates.

Birds not only symbolised the soul, sun, wind, storms, fecundity, growth, immortality but they were "fates." Certain birds had the gift of presage.

The **Crow** in Japan is a bird of ill omen. If the crow cries when anyone is ill death is near. It was looked upon as a bird of misfortune also in Italy and France:

*"Qui vous presse?    Un corbeau*
*Tout à l'heure annonçait malheur à quelque ciseau."*[1]

The **Screech Owl** was also a bird of ill omen, its
hooting bringing a sense of disaster.

In the stories of wanderings which form a part of
every myth and saga, **Birds** or **Wild Beasts** accompany
or bring aid to the heroic figure or dragon slayer.  The
bird Mimi delivers the secret to Siegfried.  "A little
bird whispered it in my ear," is still a common saying.

BAS-RELIEF OF THE BAPTISTERY OF CIVIDALE.

[1] La Fontaine's fable of *Les Deux Pigeons.*

## XVI.—SACRED ANIMALS

THE **Lion,** the most royal of beasts, typified the scorching, unrelenting, midsummer heat of the sun. As the sun-god was believed to have the power of modifying solar heat, he is often represented, as in the Samson myth, as the slayer of the lion.

**Lions in Pairs** have played an immortal part. They guarded the Sacred Tree of Life, were the guardians of doorways and temples, faced each other on the gates of cities in all countries of antiquity, and still perform the same office of watchfulness at the entrance to large public buildings, or on monuments where courage is to be extolled, even in the present day.

The **Lion** seated, showing whole figure, was the emblem of courage; showing head and shoulders only it typified force; head only with eyes open it symbolised vigilance.

**Lions** are associated with altar bases or structural

columns.  In the religious art of Egypt they act as the supporters of the sun symbol on the horizon.

The **Lion** figures prominently in mediæval church architecture, at the doors of churches and as a support to pulpits (as in the duomos of Siena, Pisa, Ravello, Lucca and elsewhere) where the symbolism of guardianship is the same.

The **Lioness** in Egypt, like the cat and vulture, typified maternity, and was given to the primitive mother goddesses who frequently have the head of a lioness.

The **Sphinx** is a form of Horus, "whose face turned eastward is the radiant sun, and whose body in the form of a lion is emblematic of his divine strength."[1] It is a symbol of royal dignity, of the power of the Pharaohs.  The Egyptians, believing that the gates of morning and evening were guarded by lion-gods; sometimes gave heads of men and women to these lion guardians which then typified the union of strength and intellect.  It was the Greeks who gave the name of "sphinxes" to these figures.  The oldest is the famous Sphinx at Gizeh.  Its age is unknown, but it existed in the time of Khephren who built the Second Pyramid (c. 4000 B.C.) and was probably very old even then.  It is supposed to be a symbol of the sun-god Ra-Temu-Khepera-Herukhuti, and the guardian and protector of the tombs about it.  In building

[1] Goodyear's *Grammar of the Lotus.*

LIONS SUPPORTING PULPIT
(Cathedral, Ravello.)

FIGURE OFFERING.  (PALACE OF
SARGON)
(Louvre, Paris.)

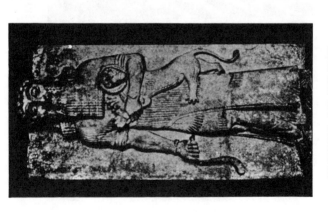

GILGAMESH AND THE LION.
(PALACE OF SARGON)
(Louvre, Paris.)

it the Egyptians were providing a "colossal abode for the spirit of the sun-god which they expected to dwell therein and protect their dead; it faced the rising sun of which it was a mighty symbol." The lion statue with a human head was called the andro-sphinx, with a ram's head the crio-sphinx. With the Greeks the sphinx was only represented in feminine form with wings and typified the pestilential heat of summer.

Among the ancients one cult identified the spirit of life with a **Bull** and another with a **Lion**. Winged human-headed lions and bulls guarded the portals of Assyrian temples.

The **Bull** symbolised the power residing in the sun. It was also a symbol of the humid side of nature and was thus given to Osiris, who besides being a sun-god, was god of the Nile and of everything that was moist, beneficent and generative in nature.

**Apis,** the bull god of the Egyptians, was believed to be an incarnation of Osiris, and an offspring of Ptah the "architect and builder of the material world." As symbolising creative force and reproductive powers, the bull-god Apis played an enormous part in the early religious worship of the Egyptians. He was searched for, examined with meticulous care, and recognised as a divine exponent by certain signs. Herodotus describes it as black, with a white square

on the forehead, a mark like an eagle on the back
and a lump like a beetle under the tongue. According
to Pliny it had a white mark shaped like a crescent
on the right side. Other authorities make the mark
on the forehead a triangle. "As the birth of Apis
filled all Egypt with joy and festivities, so his death
threw the whole country into mourning." In the
Zodiac Aries, the Celestial Ram, is the one who
breaks the icy clutch of winter and opens the way to
renewed life, and **Taurus** (the Bull) and the Sun plow
the blue meadows of the heavens. The bull like the
sun is the great fecundator of nature, and together
they symbolise the eternal productive pair. Thus the
**Bull of Heaven** found its counterpart on earth in
the **Ox.** Apis is the **Ox** into which the soul of Osiris
enters, "because the animal has been of service in
the cultivation of the ground." The connection is a
very obvious one. Osiris as a water god pours the
Nile over the land, and the bull god provided the
strength which enabled the Egyptians to plow it
up.

The bull god Apis, the Sacred Bull of the Assyrians
and the bull Nandi of the Hindus are looked upon
as identical types. Some of the numerous sculptures
represent Mithras kneeling on the back of a bull and
plunging a knife in its flank. In others he has thrown
the bull on the ground and with one knee on its
croup plunges a knife into its heart. A dog, serpent,

scorpion figure, also two youths, one with an inverted torch and the other holding aloft a burning torch. The symbolism remains a mystery.  Unless, as Frazer surmises, Mithras who was a sun-god, a corn-god, a twice-born god sacrifices the "ox who appears as a representative of the corn-spirit . . ."  The sacrificing of a bull formed a leading feature in the mysteries of Mithraism, and he suggests that the bull may be "conceived in one at least of its aspects, as an incarnation of the corn-spirit." [1]

As Mithras was the springtime sun and the Bull of the Zodiac presides over the spring, and as the ancients looked upon blood as the primary vehicle of life, it is not unjustifiable to suppose that the bull sacrificed by the sun-god was to release the waters (or blood) of life so that all nature might be revived. "From the sacrifice of the bull of Mithra the entire creation springs." [2]

Lajard finds that the two principal attributes of Venus in the Orient and Occident are the **Lion,** symbol of the sun, heat, light, the active generative power, and the **Bull,** symbol of the humid power, the passive power.  When the goddess is attended by both animals he interprets it as typifying the hermaphroditism of Venus. [3]

---

[1] Fraser's *The Golden Bough*, abridged edition, p. 468.
[2] Jung's *Psychology of the Unconscious*, Note, p. 497.
[3] *Recherches sur le Culte de Venus*, Felix Lajard.

The **Asp** was identified with the solar gods and typified the hissing, seething heat of the sun. In Egypt it was a symbol of dominion. Among the Greeks it denoted protecting or benevolent power.

The **Fish** is also associated with the sun. This may have come from an ancient conception of the universe which divided the firmament, putting the ocean below the earth and the waters of the clouds causing rains and floods above. The god of the sun passes through these as a fish or again in his sun barge.

The association of the fish, symbol of fecundity, water, the feminine principle with the sun suggests readily enough another of those ancient devices for symbolising the union of the opposite forces.

The **Dolphin,** called the "most royal of swimmers," was supposed to bear the souls of the departed to the Island of the Blessed. It was venerated by Greeks and Latins as the saviour of the shipwrecked. Thus Christ was frequently depicted as a dolphin by the early Christians.

**Two Fishes** are the zodiacal sign of Pisces. Christ is represented in the Catacombs by two fishes.

The **Fish,** because of its extraordinary fecundity, was given to Venus, also to Isis and the Japanese Kwan-non. The Christians gave it to the Virgin Mary.

In Egypt, according to Plutarch, the fish is a phallic emblem.

The **Horse** is sacred to the sun. In the Hindu Pantheon Surya, the sun, is shown drawn by seven horses with Aruna, the Dawn, as charioteer. In another representation the chariot of the Great Aum is portrayed drawn by seven *green* horses (green typifying renewal, eternal life). The ancient Greeks depicted the sun as a charioteer driving four horses across the sky. The Rhodians, who were sun worshippers, annually dedicated to the sun a chariot and four horses which they flung into the sea for his use. The Persians and Spartans sacrificed horses to the sun. In Japan a black horse was sacrificed to the god of rain.

Phœbus Apollo, the Roman god of light, is depicted in a chariot drawn by four horses. The chariot and

FROM THE CHURCH AT MARIGNY.

horses of fire which bore aloft the prophet Elijah were presumably the horses and chariot of the sun. The Kings of Judah who had forsaken Jehovah dedicated chariots and horses to the sun. Hence Josiah, renewing the covenant with the Lord, "took away the horses that the kings of Judah had given

to the sun . . . and burned the chariots of the sun
with fire." (II. Kings, 23: 11.)

The **Horse** symbolised knowledge, understanding,
intellect, wisdom. The horse sees in the dark. He is
clairvoyant and clairaudient, sees phantoms, shies,
remembers past dangers. Besides being a solar animal he symbolised the winds, and also represented
the four elements.

The cradle of the horse is in the sea. Thus Neptune
is frequently depicted sitting in a shell-shaped chariot
drawn by sea horses or dolphins, and holding his
trident in his hand.

The **White Horse** typified pure intellect, reason,
unblemished innocence, and is associated with a
Saviour-god. Buddha leaves his home on a white
horse. The Hindu Vishnu, who has incarnated in
various forms, will appear once more riding on a
white horse. The Dioscuri rode upon white horses.
St. George is pictured on a white horse. The prophecy of the second coming of Christ pictures him on
a white horse. The Four Horsemen of the Apocalypse
will be recalled.

The **Horseshoe** is an emblem of good luck and has
a protective or apotropaic meaning.

The **Horse** is also represented ridden by the devil,
and in this aspect becomes a phallic animal.

The **Ass** was the sacred animal of the Jews. Kings

judges and prophets rode on white asses. The angel of the Lord endowed Balaam's ass with the gift of speech. Christ made his entry into Jerusalem riding on an ass. The ass is sacred to Dionysos.

The Egyptians gave the ass, crocodile and hippopotamus to Typhon or Set, the principle of evil, and are said to have loathed the ass.

The **Goat** typified the reproductive powers of the sun, and is given to various solar and atmospheric gods. Thor, the Scandinavian god of thunder and fertility, is depicted in a chariot drawn by goats. The Greeks gave Pan the horns, ears and limbs of a goat.

Horus tramples under foot a **Gazelle** (called a typhonic animal). Lunar crescents are associated with gazelles. Horus holding a gazelle typifies his victory over Set.

The **Cat** was worshipped in Egypt as a form of the sun-god, and is often depicted cutting off the head of the serpent of darkness before the gods Ra, Horus, Isis. Whoever wittingly or unwittingly killed a cat was sentenced to die. When a cat died it was taken to the embalmers, its body treated with drugs and spices and then put to rest in a case carefully prepared for it. According to Plutarch, because of its nocturnal habits, its fecundity, and because the pupils of its eyes enlarge and contract with the waxing and waning of the moon, the cat also denoted the moon.

The **Baboon.** The cynocephalus or dog-headed ape plays an important part in Egyptian mythology. In the judgment scene the baboon sits upon the standard of the scales and warns Thoth when the pointer reaches the middle of the beam. Its habit of chattering the moment the sun appeared gave it the name of "Hailer of the Dawn." The baboon with uplifted paws symbolised wisdom saluting the dawn. A companion of the moon-god Thoth, it is also associated with the sun.

The **Ram** was sacred to the Egyptian sun-god of Thebes, Amen-Ra, who was depicted with a ram's

FROM A SASSANIAN BOWL.

head. In Egypt at Hermopolis, Lycopolis and Mendes the god Pan and a goat were worshipped. This is the famous Ram of Mendes, who like the Apis bull, was distinguished by certain markings. The cult, established in the second dynasty lasted till the decay of the city. There is the Ram of the Golden Fleece that was sacrificed to Zeus, and the Ram of the Zodiac, who symbolises the renewal of solar

RAM FEEDING FROM LOTUS MANGER. FIRST CENTURY A.D.
(Carnarvon Collection, Metropolitan Museum of Art.)

CYNOCEPHALUS APE. XXVI DYNASTY
(663–525 B.C.)
(Carnarvon Collection, Metropolitan
Museum of Art.)

A GAZELLE. LATE XVIII DYNASTY (1375–1350 B.C.), THEBES
(Carnarvon Collection, Metropolitan Museum of Art.)

HIPPOPOTAMUS, XXI DYNASTY
(Metropolitan Museum of Art.)

energy, is the **Celestial Ram,** the deliverer, and in this
aspect becomes the **Lamb** of Christian symbology.

**Ram's Horns** symbolised creation, or fecundity.

The **Cow** was sacred in Egypt to Hathor, Nut, Isis,
Nephthys and other nature goddesses as a symbol

ARCHAIC GREEK VASE WITH FIVE SWASTIKAS OF FOUR
DIFFERENT FORMS.

Athens.

Wilson, *The Swastika.*

of productivity. Hathor was the World Cow, typifying fertility. In Greece the cow was sacred to
Hera whose car in religious processions is drawn by
oxen. The Cow is the symbol of the Great Mother.

It was worshipped by the Hindus and is still revered in India.

The **Frog** was a symbol among the Egyptians of the watery elements or primordial slime. Each of the four primeval gods (Heh, Kek, Nau, Amen), were represented with the head of a frog. Their feminine counterparts were serpent headed. This is one of the oldest cults in Egypt.

The **Panther or Leopard** was said to allure men, beasts and cattle by the sweetness of its breath. It

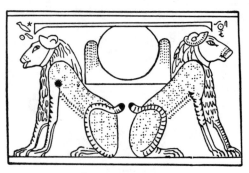

EGYPTIAN LION GODS "YESTERDAY AND TO-DAY" SUPPORTING SOLAR DISK.

is the symbolic animal of Dionysos and was sacred in Egypt to Osiris, who is frequently depicted as a crouching leopard with above him the open eye symbol, or he has near him the spotted skin of the leopard. These spots like eyes symbolised the Great Watcher.

The **Dog** was called by the Egyptians Hermes, because the philosophic character of the animal typified the most logical of the gods. The early Greek writers all testify to the sacred character of the dog in Egypt and the myth of the dog as companion and assistant to the gods, which is also found among the Persians and Hindus, probably goes back to the worship of the jackal or dog-headed god Anubis who is the Egyptian Hermes.

# XVII.—ANCIENT GODS AND GODDESSES

THE confused and contradictory ideas that the centuries have piled up, the ragged glimpses of inconsistencies that even mysticism cannot explain—(yet always a gleam of something higher) make the ancient religions of Egypt and Babylonia as involved and puzzling as they are fascinating. Especially is this true of Egypt.

Roeder in his *Symbol Psychology*,[1] referring to the recurrence of typical stories in all countries and among all peoples, instances the universal saga of the hero, who as he sets forth, is usually alone except for an animal companion, then with multitudes, then with a select few (the chosen few of the Jews, Christ's disciples, King Arthur and his Round Table, etc.), then these drop away and the hero of the legend dies alone.

The story of the gods seems to represent also this eternal law of progression from unity to multiplicity and back to unity again.

Out of Chaos (the feminine principle who is the Mother of all the Gods) comes the first manifestation of life. Tiamat is the Babylonian Chaos Demon,

[1] Adolph Roeder, *Symbol Psychology*.

the primeval ocean "from whose fertile depths came every living thing." She was the Great Mother and

MARDUK THE CHIEF BABYLONIAN DEITY.
From Jastrow.

also the dragon of the sea whom Marduk the solar god destroys. The Egyptian Neith is also a Virgin Mother self-produced and self-sustaining, the Unknown One, the Hidden One, the personification of the feminine principle of life, who was believed to have brought forth Ra, the Lord of all Light, the Mighty Sun.

Although Neith is called an earth-goddess the Egyptians seem to have considered the sky feminine and the earth masculine, but this may have been before they had divided up the universe between them or before Woman had had an opportunity to display those diverse qualities that have given her such unexpected and alluring charm and made her such a piquant associate on the long journey through life.

Nut, too, is a heaven-goddess, Seb the earth-god and Shu, whose symbol is a feather, is the air or space which divides them.

Thus, the Egyptians sometimes represent the sky as a great cow, standing with its four legs on the four corners of the earth.

Hathor the ubiquitous, universal World Mother is the great cow-goddess.

Among the Semites the Baal (god, lord, owner) was identified with the reproductive power of water and the Baalath, or feminine energy, with the earth.

In the countries where the sun scorches and devastates, the moon was reverenced as the higher power. Thus in the more primitive religions Osiris has been interpreted as the moon-god and his brother Typhon or Set, who is the evil principle, is the sun.

The Great Mother was looked upon as the higher principle among the Egyptians and mother deities abound.  Mut is a great World Mother who wears the united crowns of North and South, holds the

OSIRIS
(Metropolitan Museum
of Art.)

NEITH, WEARING CROWN OF
LOWER EGYPT
(Metropolitan Museum
of Art.)

THOTH
(Metropolitan Museum
of Art.)

PTAH
(Metropolitan Museum
of Art.)

*crux ansata* in one hand and the papyrus sceptre in the other.

Nekhebet was a vulture-goddess, Uatchet a serpent-goddess.

Nut the sky-goddess is a primeval mother and associated with Neith, Mut and Hathor. Maat is the goddess of truth and her symbol is a feather.

As the one who dispenses life, the great Mother-goddess represented nature under her two-fold aspect prolific and destructive by turns, yet she was eternal and undecaying, "being the goddess of the land."

Recognising the eternity of matter, it was the "self-power" or life in nature—in trees, rivers, hills, vegetation, animals—that the ancients worshipped as manifestations of a Divine, Unknown Power.

Gods multiplied, shifted with changing thought. Besides the great gods of sun and moon, fire and water and earth, there were atmospheric gods of winds, storms, lightning, rain; the vegetation gods who are tree spirits, corn spirits; the secondary gods of fire—Ptah, Vulcan, Hephæstos—gods who forge the thunderbolts; gods of wisdom and counsel, Thoth, Minerva, Athene; the messenger gods, Anubis, Hermes—a vast multitude of deities grafted on from time to time, yet as typifying forces of nature they meant in all countries of antiquity practically the same thing.

All are given animals. The high gods have the

lion, bull, goat, eagle, falcon, symbols of solar creative
energy.　Zeus　has　the　eagle,　Brahma　the　goose,

ADAD THE GOD OF STORMS.
From Jastrow's *Civilization of Babylonia and Assyria.*

Horus is the falcon-god, Amen Ra of Thebes has
the ram.　Marduk, the sun-god of the Babylonians,
has the goat and the lion.　Ashur, the mighty sun-
god of the Assyrians, has the lion and eagle and is
also the "bull of heaven," the bull in this instance
typifying the power that resides in the sun, or possibly the "self-power" of the god who is thought to
combine the creative forces in himself.　Thor, the

god of thunder, is depicted in a chariot drawn by goats. Odin has two ravens and two dogs. The lesser gods are given the animal that best suits their characteristics. Anubis is the jackal-headed or dog-headed god. Hermes has many animals sacred to him—the tortoise, cock, ram, goat. In a drawing by Raphael he is depicted in a chariot drawn by cocks. The same artist depicts Venus in a chariot drawn by doves. The Egyptian Bast was a feline goddess. In Scandinavia Freija, the goddess who presides over smiling nature, is depicted in a car drawn by cats. All feline goddesses represent the variable power of the sun as reflected in nature. The serpent, lioness, vulture, cow were given to the goddesses of maternity and productivity. The Greek Aphrodite has the sparrow, swan, swallow, dove, dolphin, hare, tortoise, ram, and when it is wished to typify the hermaphroditism of the goddess she is given the lion and bull. Artemis, the "huntress among the immortals," is given dogs, stags and the boar. Four stags with golden antlers draw her chariot. This association of the gods with birds and animals forms an epic in itself and one of far too great moment and beauty to be more than suggested here.

In Egypt the gods are duplicated and re-duplicated. It was said to be less difficult to find a god than a man. Flinders Petrie explains this: "Polytheism was

the result of the mixture of families and Tribes . . .
the polytheism is really the tribal history fossilised.
There was no idea of a jealous god, no one worship
excluded another, each was considered true for its
own place and people." [1]

In the Mother cult the male god is the husband,
son or lover. In the Father cult the goddess is recognised, but is subordinate to the male. Under a cen-
tralised government the two cults were merged in
Egypt, however, long before history begins. And the
coming together of people of widely divergent tastes
and ideas, and the insensible fusing of religious beliefs
produces a most complex and contradictory mythology.

There are many confusing lapses. Younger gods
displace older gods, yet father and son are identical.
Both represent phases of the One who is the Supreme
Power. Osiris is the sun at night. Horus, his son, is
the fresh morning sun. Christ says *I and my Father
are one* and it was a Hindu belief that a man is
literally reborn in the person of his son.

In time, as in the universal saga of the hero, the
company becomes more select. The Supreme Power,
the great sun-god absorbs the attributes of the lesser
gods. He is the one great god, the god of might.
He is Marduk of Babylon, the Mysterious One, the
"lord of many existences," he who is unknown to

[1] *The God of Ancient Egypt*, W. M. Flinders Petrie.

mankind and who died to give birth to human life;
he is Ashur of Assyria, the God of Gods, the embodiment of the genius of Assyria; he is Ra of Egypt,
"the ONE god who came into being in the beginning
of time" and in whose worship even that of the
powerful mother goddess is merged.

And now at last flashing on the horizon come the
immortal pair—the pair that touch the imagination.

Known in Egypt as Isis and Osiris, in Babylonia
as Ishtar and Tammuz, in Phrygia as Attis and
Cybele and in Greece Adonis and Aphrodite, for
the first time you feel the closer relationship, feel that
each is essential to the other. For the first time you
are given a glimpse of love. When Osiris is killed by
the treachery of his brother Set, it is Isis who searches
everywhere over the length and breadth of Egypt
until she finds her husband's body and restores it to
life. Ishtar, mourning and inconsolable, descends to
the nether regions searching for her lover, the youthful sun-god Tammuz, and all vegetation dies during
her absence. Cybele mourns for the slain Attis.
Aphrodite, hastening to her wounded lover, Adonis,
treads on a bush of white roses. Thorns tear her
tender flesh, and her blood stains the roses forever red.

Time goes on. There are other changes—a complete shifting of thought.

The sun that has enlarged imagination, and the serene, untroubled moon are still in the heavens shining down upon mankind, but no longer as gods —no longer as bride and bridegroom. The sun, the hero of a thousand adventures, of a thousand amours, the Great Lover of romance who trifles even with Mother Earth, is now only a "huge globular mass of flaming gases."

.     .     .     .     .

The legend is finished.   The gods are myths.
"The Great Pan is dead."
All that is left are their symbols that they so faithfully cherished, and that we still see them holding as we visit museums and ancient temples—the *crux ansata*, the trisula, cross, triangle, circle—all the old symbols of life.

## XVIII.—THE TWICE-BORN GODS

*"The gods might die annually. The goddesses alone were immortal."*

As they featured the drama of the universe, the younger gods of vegetation, gods of fertility, storm, fire, gradually assume solar attributes and become twice-born gods. They are the spring sun-gods and fire-gods. The Phrygian Attis, the youthful Tammuz of the Babylonians, the Greek Adonis and the Egyptian Osiris represented the yearly decay and the renewal of life—more especially the life of all nature and vegetation, which they personified as gods who died annually, and then rose again from the dead. Dionysos is a twice-born god. In a painting at Pompeii he is depicted as a solar deity with his symbolic animal, the panther. Again as a solar god he is pictured seated on a sun globe strewn with stars.

Mithra is also identified with the Greek god Dionysos and all the other twice-born gods of regeneration, and each is said to be born on December 25th for it is then that the sun is born, the winter solstice is ended, and the great god of light pursues once more his revivifying journey northward.

In this mighty pageant the sun was represented as the Creator, the twelve months his attendants, the twelfth month his betrayer through whom he meets his doom. He descends into the abode of death only to rise again in the full glory of light and power for the eternal salvation of mankind.

From the death and resurrection of Osiris the Egyptians drew all their hope of eternal life. "As Osiris lives, so shall he also live; as Osiris died not, so shall he also not die; as Osiris perished not, so shall he also not perish."

Dying to live was, as we have seen, the keystone of all ancient religions and each year as spring returned all nature revived this faith in the immortality of life.

The various Mysteries—of which the Orphic, the Eleusinian, those of Cybele and Attis and of the dead and risen Adonis or Tammuz are the most famous, were originally vernal festivals in celebration of the return to life of nature.

In like manner the vernal festivals of the pagans, celebrating the resurrection of the generative powers of nature are reflected again in the springtime festival of Easter in celebration of the dead and risen Christ.

That these ancient myths and customs gradually became an integral part of the Christian religion is not surprising, although it forms one of the most

interesting and unusual chapters in the development
of religions. We may assume, even though he con-
tradicts us, that what makes the Christian shudder
is his own abysmal inconsistency, which he has spent
nearly two thousand years in furious contentions
trying to explain away. It was the avowed purpose
of the early Christians to break down nature worship,
which in a profligate age, had degenerated into licentious rites as indecent as they were corrupting. By
their implacable persistency, the Christians succeeded
in closing the temples and destroying the gods.
Their mistake in not being able to dissociate a degenerate form of worship from the object worshipped,
has dogged them ever since. The Church itself soon
saw that neither religions nor human beings can
separate themselves from God's highest revelation to
man and live; that to be in tune with the Infinite
one must be subtly, mystically in tune with nature
which throbs and vibrates to the harmonies of Life.
And so one by one the Church slipped the old pagan
rites, that the hearts of the people craved, into her
ritual. In response to the desire for a visible semblance, she established saints and wayside shrines.
In response to the passionate longing for the adorable
feminine principle, the Church in the middle ages
elevated the Great Mother again in the person of the
Virgin Mother of Christ.[1] The Church did this

[1] See *Life Symbols*, pp. 341–6.

silently, skilfully—wisely bowing to the inevitable. Only those adherents who tried to explain as a divine miracle what was merely a common-sense adjustment to the Law of Life were left gasping, and later became protesting protestants (still protesting) while the Church knowing, although she cannot explain it logically, that she is one with life goes her serene way.

**Fire,** as we have seen, played a large part in the ritual of the sun-worshippers.[1] Besides using it to aid the god in his struggle with winter and death, it

became in itself a means of purification, of renewal. In order that the reigning power, like the sun, might be ever young and glorious, there came about the annual burning of kings, or their effigies—or men were chosen by lot to impersonate the king and become the sacrifice. This, too, became a pageant. The beggar who was king for a day or four days, as

[1] See *Life Symbols*, pp. 186–93.

the case might be, was invested with all the trappings and power of royalty. To make the sacrifice more impressive he was frequently chosen for his beauty and physical perfection. All knees bent to him. He had his moment, then passes on. Dramas are still fashioned on this ancient motif, this old theme of King for a Day.

## XIX.—TRIADS AND THE TRIANGLE

 **The Triangle,** the geometrical emblem of three things, one above two, the two lower uniting to produce the higher, or the union of the positive and negative forces to produce the third, is the most complex and mystical, as it is the most uncompromising of all symbols.

Beginning with chaos, then unity or the self-created, there comes duality—and man's thoughts are no sooner ensnared by that, for he is so made that he loves his opposite, than a third force presents itself, which is the result or life.—*"Pere, mère et fils (essence, substance et vie)."*

From earliest times primitive man appears to have grasped the idea of the three-fold nature of the universe—the divine, the human, the natural world—and that he himself was the image or mirror of the macrocosm, composed of three things—body, mind, soul or spirit. The idea of "three in one" seems to have been a part of man's consciousness as far back as tradition takes us.

The **Triangle** was used by primordial man at first

presumably as a race symbol signifying the family—
father, mother, child. "The Egyptian temples were
dedicated to three gods. The first the male principle,
the second the female, and the third the offspring of
the other two, but these three are blended into one."

From the Trinity of the family and the multitude
of triads in nature arose, we may suppose, the conception of a trinity of gods. It is significant that the
most ancient religions contain such triads or family
groups.

THE PENTACLE.

SOLOMON'S SEAL.

The magic of the number three has piqued both
mystics and philosophers. The reason of its mystical
significance still eludes us, unless as Pythagoras is so
often quoted as saying "God works everywhere by
geometry," and Flammarion in our own day con-
cludes that "in everything and everywhere numbers
rule the world." [1]

**Three** has been called the very soul of magic,
astrology, divination. "Even its use is three-fold,
one definite showing intrinsic value, the other sym-

[1] *Popular Astronomy*, Camille Flammarion, p. 225.

bolic, esoteric, and the third indefinite signifying many."

Thrice was the Greek equivalent for many times. We demand three cheers. Thought instinctively groups itself in threes:—(Birth, life, death, sun, moon, stars; sky, earth, water). There is apparently something inexpressibly compelling in the very cadence, the way the voice or thought, suspended on two, pauses in fulfillment on three.

Aristotle's definition is a familiar one:—"The triad is the number of the complete whole, inasmuch as it contains a beginning, a middle and an end."

Thus **two** among the ancients represented contention, the opposites, and **three** symbolised completion, the rounded totality of life. It was called the first perfect number. "A man is perfect when he consists of three, himself, his wife and his son." (Rigveda vii, 3.)

**Three Pillars** typifying Wisdom, Strength, Beauty, or Wisdom, Power, Goodness were used to symbolise their triune gods by the very early Egyptians, Hindus, Druids, Mayas and Incas.

Set, Horus and Shu, a primary Egyptian trinity, were symbolised by a triangle enclosed in a circle. In the earlier mythology, Horus was the water season, Set was the drought, the destroyer, and Shu the god of winds and storms, was the reconciler and mediator.

STELA OF HORUS ON
THE CROCODILES
HOLDING EVIL
CREATURES IN
HIS HANDS AND
SURMOUNTED
BY THE GOD
BES. PTOL-
E M A I C
PERIOD
(Metropolitan
Museum of
Art.)

THOTH PRESENTING THE CRUX ANSATA TO THE FALCON GOD HORUS
(Metropolitan Museum of Art.)

APIS BULL
(Metropolitan Museum of Art.)

QUEEN SITRA AND KING RAMESES MAKING OFFERINGS BEFORE OSIRIS,
ISIS AND HATHOR, ABYDOS.  XIX DYNASTY
(Metropolitan Museum of Art.)

Shu, too, was the god who first lifted the heavens from the earth in the form of a Triangle and he is depicted standing on seven steps within a Triangle.

In Egyptian sun worship Dawn, noon, sunset represented "three in one of the sacred substance of the sun as three divine persons existed perpetually in the substance of uncreated Light." Thus the heat and glow of the noonday sun represented Ra. The sun going down typified Osiris. In the morning sun Osiris lives again in the incarnate Horus.

There were innumerable triads in Egypt that personified the chief forces of nature under different groupings. In time, however, Osiris, Isis and Horus absorbed the functions and attributes of all the other gods and became the mightiest gods of Egypt. Osiris was the Sun and Isis the Moon. Osiris was called the brother, husband, son of Isis. Originally a Virgin Mother and Horus her fatherless son, the marriage of Isis with Osiris and his adoption of Horus is a later adaptation. In the worship of this powerful triad we see the gradual trend towards monotheism or unity. Osiris was a moon-god, a solar-god, a water-god. Fused with Ra the sun-god he died each day as an old man, appearing in heaven as the constellation Orion which was his ghost. He was the god and judge of the dead. He was the bi-sexual Nile spirit, the Apis bull, the Ram of Mendes—whatever represented growth, energy, the generative power of nature.  But above all Osiris was worshipped by the Egyptians as the *god-man* who suffered, died, rose again from the dead to reign forever in the heavens.  Isis, too, absorbed all the characteristics of the other goddesses. She was the Great Mother, a sky and water goddess, the earth goddess, the moon goddess.  She stood for all things that are high and fine and good.[1]  It has been said that but for her presence in Egypt the world would never have known a madonna.  She is the Eternal Feminine.  She is "Isis veiled: 'I am all that has been, all that is, and all that will be and no mortal has drawn aside my veil'."  In the mystical cult Osiris was the power of light, reason, intellect.  Isis was the

[1] "Her attributes and epithets are so numerous that in the hieroglyphics she is called 'the many-named,' 'the thousand-named.' . . .  The true wife, the tender mother, the beneficent queen of nature, encircled with the nimbus of moral purity, of immemorial and mysterious sanctity. . . .  In that welter of religions which accompanied the decline of national life in antiquity, her worship was one of the most popular in Rome and throughout the empire. . . .  In a period of decadence . . . when the fabric of empire itself, once deemed eternal, began to show ominous rents and fissures, the serene figure of Isis with her spiritual calm, her gracious promise of immortality appeared to many like a star in a stormy sky . . . and roused in their breasts a rapture of devotion not unlike that paid in the Middle Ages to the Virgin Mary. . . .  Her stately ritual with its shaven and tonsured priests, its matins and vespers, its tinkling music, its baptism and aspersions of holy water, its solemn procession, its jewelled images of the Mother of God, presented many points of similarity to the pomps and ceremonies of Catholicism." Fraser's *The Golden Bough*, abridged edition, pp. 382-3.

power of matter, the receptive, the nurse, the all
mother, and Horus, born from this union of spirit
(or reason) and matter is the "sensible image of the
mental world."

Anu, Enlil and Ea were the early Babylonian triad
and Ea the god of water is the "beneficent one, the
mediator who is constantly on the side of humanity."
In a later triad Babylon the "mother of astronomy,
star worship and astrology . . . influenced by theo-
logical speculations" worshipped Sin the moon-god,
then Shamash the sun, and Ishtar as the planet
Venus. Even when the Assyrians placed Ashur,
their sun-god, at the head of the pantheon, they
included the powerful and potent Ishtar, the goddess
of fertility, whom we have seen as Mother Earth
mourning for the lost sun-god, Tammuz. It is the
same Ishtar who when associated with the heroic
Ashur becomes the goddess of war, and with the
beloved Tammuz is the goddess of vegetation and
as the planet Venus is the Queen of Heaven, the
'rival of the sun and moon.' Far less spiritual than
Isis "Ishtar is the goddess of human instinct or passion which accompanies human love. She is the
mother of mankind—but also she who awakens human
passion. . . . Seven centuries after the religion of
Assyria and Babylonia had passed out, leaving scarcely
a trace, the Romans brought Cybele, the Phrygian

Mother goddess, and built a temple to her honour. It was Ishtar of Babylonia transformed to meet changed conditions, the same great feminine principle of nature in its various manifestations, as mother earth the source of all fertility at once the loving mother of mankind and of the gods."[1]

In the Zoroastrian triad Ahura Mazda (Ormuzd) is the sun—or power of light, life, heaven, good, Ahrimanes is the power of darkness, evil, death, the earth, matter; and Mithra is the god of sunlight, the power of Truth, the Mediator between heaven and earth.

In the Hindu triad Brahma is the Creator, Vishnu the Preserver, Siva the Destroyer or Apathy. In the Buddhist triad Buddha is intelligence, the soul, the generative power; Dharma is matter, the body, the productive power; and Sangha represents the union of the two. (From this union, or as a result of this union Sangha becomes the author of creation.)

Although the Chinese divided nature into the two great parts *Yang* and *Yin* it was by the co-operation of these two that Life or the third or neuter principle was evolved.

The grouping of gods in three represented a very early phase of the Greek religion. The three sons of Saturn were Jupiter (Zeus), the god of heaven; Neptune (Poseidon), the god of the sea; and Pluto

[1] Jastrow's *Religious Belief in Babylonia and Assyria.*

or Hades, the god of the lower world. The three great deities of the Greeks, however, were Zeus, Hera and Poseidon, who are identified with the Roman Jupiter, Juno and Neptune. The student will recall many others. These have been briefly touched upon only to show how possessed man has been by the idea of "three in one" which was to be used again in the Christian religion in that superbly mystical conception (so tortured by those who would explain it literally) of God the Father, the Son and the Holy Ghost.

In adopting the ancient idea of a Trinity in Unity they also adopted as its symbol the equilateral triangle, an emblem so old, so universal, so widespread that its origin is lost in that unfathomable past, that so reluctantly delivers its secrets.

The **Triangle,** as we have seen in the symbols of the elements, was used to typify fire.

Two interlacing triangles forming a six-pointed star represented the two chief forces of nature, fire which flames up and water which flows down. It thus became a perfect androgynous symbol of the two forces that create life, the triangle with point upward typifying fire or the masculine force, and that with the apex below, water, or the passive principle. This same form is also the **Hexagram** or **Solomon's Seal** with which he was said to have worked miracles. Sometimes the lower triangle is dark and the upper one light, typifying the union of the spiritual and material, or spirit and matter.

The **Triangle** is called a primary form of the pyramid. "The royal mind that conceived the pyramids and intended them to endure as everlasting monuments to the entrance and exit of a human career, undoubtedly felt the stability of the three sided figure."

The **Triangle** is one of the symbols of the Buddhist triad. In the secret doctrines of certain sects it typified the *yoni* or matrix "from which the world was manifest." In Japan it is a flame symbol typifying fire. The Egyptians called the nature of the universe the fairest of triangles. The form that signified the feminine principle or maternity was the hieroglyph of the moon, and is often depicted with the sacred baboon. Sometimes the triangle surmounts a pillar with the baboon before it in an attitude of worship.

The **Triangle** was the delight of the Greek philosophers. Plato used it as a symbol of marriage. In this triangle he makes the perpendicular equal three, the base four and the hypothenuse five. The perpendicular represents the male, the base the female and the hypothenuse their offspring. This is Osiris the first principle, Isis the matrix and Horus the completed world, for "three is the first odd number and is perfect, four is a square that has an even number—two—for its side and five is in some respects like each parent for it is the sum of three and two." In this diagram of marriage Plato calls the son "that which is better."

The Pythagoreans adopted the **Triangle** as the most perfect geometrical figure, inasmuch as it was the first form complete in itself.

**The Triangle enclosed by a Circle** is thus defined by Plutarch: "The area within this Triangle is the common hearth of them all and is named the 'Plain of Truth' in which the Reason, the forms and the patterns of all things that have been, and that shall be, are stored up not to be disturbed; and as Eternity dwells around them, from thence time like a stream from a fountain flows down upon the worlds."[1]

And here having followed this fascinating pair—Man and Woman—to where they are no longer two but three, here we leave them in Plutarch's "Plain of Truth."

These ancient symbols that have existed so long, covered such a large part of the earth's surface, impressed themselves so permanently on art, architecture, music, mathematics, astronomy, religion reveal

[1] Plutarch's *On the Cessation of Oracles.*

—and the revelation is astoundingly clear—that man, that paradox of good and evil was never without ideals. There is, it is true, the same paradox in these old symbols of life. They can indicate everything that the depraved imagination, or the literal ones incapable of imagination may desire, yet there they stand, immutable, unchanging, speaking clearly from a far off past of the cross, creative energy; the circle, perfection; the serpent, the means of combining creative energy and perfection; the triangle, the result, the ultimate realisation of multiplicity in unity, of three in one; and the Three Pillars, Wisdom, Strength, Beauty, the eternal goal.

# XX.—SOME GENERAL SYMBOLS AND SYMBOLIC FIGURES FOUND IN EARLY ART

**Acacia.** A mystical symbol remarkable for its reproductive powers and used by the Egyptians in their capitals and thence borrowed by the Greeks.

**Adonis.** The mother of Adonis was fabled to have been changed into a tree which at the end of nine months burst, and Adonis was born. The story of his being found as an infant by Aphrodite and concealed in a chest which the goddess gave to Persephone who refused to give him up until Zeus, appealed to by Aphrodite commanded that Adonis spend six months with each, is simply a variant of the Babylonian myth of Ishtar and Tammuz. Adonis grows up into a beautiful youth, is the beloved of Aphrodite who shares with him the pleasures of the chase. One legend relates that Ares (Mars) jealous of Aphrodite's love for him transformed himself into a wild boar and killed him. Others represent Adonis as being carried off by Dionysos. Another tells of Aphrodite rushing to the spot where her lover was wounded and sprinkling his blood with nectar from which flowers sprang up. In one myth Aphrodite changes him into a flower. Scarlet anemones were said to have sprung from the blood of Adonis. One of the loveliest myths is that the red rose owes its hue to the death of Adonis. Aphrodite hastening to her wounded lover trod on a bush of white roses. The thorns tore her tender flesh and stained the roses forever red. Worship of Adonis is thought to have originated in Phœnicia spreading from there to Assyria, Egypt, Greece and Italy. In the Asiatic cults Aphrodite is the fructifying principle in nature and Adonis the twice-born god who dies in winter and is revived in the spring. The festivals of Adonis were celebrated in Athens, Alexandria, Byblus and many other places.

**Aegis.** The shield of Zeus or Athene with the Gorgon's head in the centre. Later it came to mean the breast-plate worn by emperors and others.

**Agni (ignis).** The Hindu god of the moving flame, at times beneficent and again destructive.

**Almond.** A symbol of virginity and self-production, also fruitfulness. The mystical *Vesica Piscis* surrounding the Virgin Mary in some representations in art is derived from the *mandorla*, almond—and is used to convey the same symbolic idea. Candied almonds with a white coating and distributed in boxes to each guest is a part of the ritual of Italian weddings. The almond is also identified with the *yoni* of phalli-

# Ancient Pagan Symbols 157

cism. "In Phrygian cosmogony an almond figured
as the father of all things perhaps because its delicate
lilac blossom is one of the first heralds of spring."[1]

**Ambrosia Vase.** In Chinese art this was originally
a dish held in the hand of a god to catch the dew of
heaven. In the hands of Kwan-yin it is long-necked
and used to sprinkle the water of life on worshippers.
Sometimes the vase rests on a stand beside the goddess who holds in her hand the willow branch.

**Amentet.** It was during the journey of the deceased
through *Amentet*, the Hidden Place that he came in
contact with the gods and "invoked the powers of
the amulets with which they were so closely connected."

**Ammon or Amen the Hidden One.** A sun-god of
Thebes whose worship extended until as Amen-Ra he
became the national deity of Egypt. He is represented as a man wearing the lofty double plumes
and holds the sceptre, the *crux ansata* and sometimes
the *Khepesh* or war knife; sometimes he has the head
of a hawk with the solar disk and uræus, and before
him the *crux ansata* or *ankh* which has been given
arms and legs and is offering him lotus flowers; or
again he has the head of a ram, crocodile or lion with
the disk, plumes and uræi. He has even been represented in the form of the solar goose. He was usually
depicted, however, with a ram's head, symbol of

[1] Fraser's *Adonis, Attis, Osiris*, p. 219.

creative energy, and was known as the ram-headed god of the sun.

**Amorini.** A name given to the small Cupids or little love-gods that are frequently found in the decorative art of all ages.

**Amphora.** A two-handled Greek vase, usually of large size and intended to hold liquids. Some were mounted on a foot, others not. The prize to the victors in the Panathenaic games was an amphora.

**Amulet.** A word derived from the East and applied to various objects or "charms" which, when worn, were supposed to ward off illnesses and evil influences and bring good luck to the wearer.

**Anubis or Anpu.** The jackal or dog-headed god Anubis is the Egyptian Hermes. He is called the Opener of the Ways. He is the messenger, custodian and servant of the gods, and the conductor of souls to the promised land. Anubis was said to be the son of Osiris and performs the service of watching over Isis and Osiris. In the temples he is represented as the guard and protector of the other gods. The place in front of the temple was sacred to Anubis. Again the horizon was called Anubis and depicted in the form of a dog because the dog sees both by day and night. The jackal, a species of wild dog was reputed to hunt up the lion's prey for him. Thus Anubis, originally the jackal type, is later represented with the dog as emblem. The confusion in term may be attributed to the growth or domestication of an idea. Jackal in Egypt denoted judge and it was probably the jackal god who ministered to Osiris and acted as guide to the nether world.

**Anvil.** Symbol of the "Primal Furnace," the Force which helped to hammer out the Universe.

**Aphrodite (Venus).** "As unmoral as nature itself but not immoral." The goddess of love and beauty was said by some to have sprung from the foam of the sea. A personification of the generative powers of nature she was called the mother of all living beings. Wife of Hephæstos she does not scruple to have amours with Ares, Poseidon, Dionysos and Hermes among the gods, and inspired by Zeus she also conceived an invincible passion for Anchises, a mortal. Her love for Adonis has been interpreted as the myth of the changing seasons. She was reputed to be the mother of Priapus by Dionysos and of Hermaphroditus by Hermes. Aphrodite has a magic girdle which cannot fail to inspire love for those who wear it. The sparrow, swan, swallow, dove, dolphin, hare, tortoise and ram were sacred to her. She was given also the apple, poppy, myrtle and rose. She is associated with the planet Venus and the month of April and the numbers three, four and seven are sacred to her. Sacrifices offered to her were mostly garlands of flowers and incense. The worship of Aphrodite was derived from the East where she is identified with

Astarte and the biblical Ashtoreth. As the victorious
goddess she has the helmet, shield and sword and
sometimes an arrow. She is sometimes draped but
in the later period she is nude.

**Apollo.** A Greek god who was identified with Helios
or the sun and also with the Egyptian Horus. He
is the god of light who at his birth destroys Python,
the serpent of darkness. He typified also mental
light and presided over knowledge, music, poetry and
eloquence. Apollo was the national divinity of the
Greeks "reflecting the brightest side of the Greek
mind." He is the protector of flocks and herds, the
god of the bow and arrows, who punishes and destroys
the wicked and wards off evil, he is the god of prophecy
and his most famous oracles were at Delos, Delphi,
Branchidæ, Claros and Patara. The finest temple
to Apollo was at Delphi. In art he is represented as
the "perfect ideal of youthful manliness." As god
of music he holds the lyre and is depicted draped or
with long, flowing locks. Again he holds the bow and
arrow. His symbols are the wolf, raven, swan, lyre
and laurel, etc. The number seven was sacred to him.

**Archer.** The Assyrian deity Ashur is represented
as an archer shooting a three-headed arrow at the
enemies of Assyria. Sagittarius is the archer of the
zodiac.

**Ares (Mars).** Whereas Athene represented wisdom
and foresight in the conduct of war, Ares is the god

of force who typifies the horrors, tumult, confusion of war. He was one of the lovers of Aphrodite and when she transferred her affections to Adonis, Ares waylaid him in the form of a wild boar and killed him. The wolf, cock and woodpecker are sacred to Ares.

**Ariadne.** A daughter of Minos, King of Crete. Falling in love with Theseus who had been sent from Athens to Crete to be devoured by the Minotaur, she gave him the string by which he found his way out of the labyrinth. Her legends vary. In one she marries and goes away with Theseus who deserts her, whereupon she takes her own life. In another she is killed by Artemis. In others Dionysos enamoured of her beauty raised her to the rank of the immortals and gave her a crown of seven stars. Ariadne was called a serpent goddess and is frequently represented in art and on ancient coins and gems usually with serpents. Theseus and the labyrinth are interpreted as solar.

**Artemis (Diana).** One of the great divinities of the Greeks known under many aspects. Called by some a daughter of Zeus by Leto and sister of Apollo, others call her the daughter of Demeter. An Egyptian account makes her the daughter of Dionysos and Isis. As sister of Apollo who was identified with the sun or Helios she becomes a moon goddess and like Apollo is armed with a bow, quiver and arrows and has the power to send plagues and death to men and animals.

Like Apollo, too, she is unmarried. She is the "chaste Diana," the maiden unconquered by love. She is the protector of the young, of flocks and herds and the chase. As the Arcadian Artemis she is goddess of the nymphs. Hephæstos makes her bow and arrows, and Pan provides her with dogs. As a nymph, fish were sacred to her and Artemis and Apollo both have the laurel. Among the symbolic animals of the Greek Artemis were dogs, stags and the boar. In Greek art when depicted as huntress she has the bow and arrows or spear, dogs and stags. As the moon goddess she wears a long robe and has the moon crescent above her head. Sometimes she carries a torch. The Tauri, a people of European Sarmatia, sacrificed all strangers to Artemis. The worship of the goddess was orgiastic and it is believed that this was originally an Asiatic moon goddess whom the Greeks confused with their own Artemis. Aricia was the seat of her worship in Italy where she was known as Diana and also called Trivia when worshipped at cross-ways where her statues were usually placed. The Ephesian Artemis is an Asiatic goddess of nature whom the Greeks found in Ionia and to whom they gave the name of Artemis. As goddess of fertility she is many breasted, wears a mural crown with disk as emblem of the full moon, her legs are swathed like a mummy, the lower part of her body ending in a point like a pyramid upside down and covered with mystical figures of bees, flowers, bulls and stags. The pine cone was sacred to Artemis, [see pine cone], also the cypress or fir tree. The symbol of the Ephesian Artemis was a bee.

**Athene (Minerva).** One of the great divinities of the Greeks and said to have sprung in full armour from the head of Zeus. She is a goddess in whom "power and wisdom are harmoniously blended" and typified the ethical rather than some physical aspect of nature, thus differing from the great mother goddesses of earth and sky. She is a virgin goddess removed from the passions of love and hate. She is the goddess of wisdom, war and all the liberal arts. She could hurl the thunderbolt, prolong the life of men and bestow the gift of prophecy. As goddess of war and protector of heroes she is usually represented in armour with the ægis and a golden staff. In ancient art she is frequently given a helmet ornamented with ram's heads, griffins, sphinxes and horses, or again with the ægis and sometimes a shield which has in its centre the head of Medusa. The owl, serpent, cock, lance and olive branch are her symbols. The olive in allusion to the fact that she was said to have created the olive tree in her contest with Poseidon for the possession of Attica. She was the Roman Minerva and was also called Pallas and Tritonia.

**Ba.** The Egyptians represented the *ba* or soul by

a bird, sometimes with a human head. There was also the luminous one or *Khou* which hid itself in the darkest corner of the vault.

**Bacchus.** Called by the Greeks Lord of the Palm Tree. [See Dionysos.]

**Ball or Tama.** A symbol among the Buddhists of the sacred emanations of the gods. It is sometimes surmounted by flames and is called the "flaming jewel" or "flaming pearl." It is the third eye of Buddha, the symbol of transcendent wisdom.

**Basilisk.** A fabulous creature with the body and wings of a dragon, head of a serpent and tail ending in a serpent's head. The glance of its eye would kill. It could only be destroyed by holding a mirror up so that it must see itself, when it would burst asunder with horror of its own appearance. We have here the same thought of the Taoists about evil being made to recognise itself. In sacred art the basilisk was used to symbolise the spirit of evil.

**Bee.** Vishnu when depicted in the form of Krishna was given a blue bee hovering over his head as a symbol of the ether. Carved on ancient tombs the bee symbolised immortality. The bee was a prominent feature of the Mithra cult. On an altar dedicated to the Persian sun-god was found a gilded bull's head and three hundred golden bees. Napoleon I. adopted the bee as an emblem of sovereignty. The sanctity of the bee may be derived from the ancient custom

of smearing the bodies of the dead with honey to
prevent decomposition.

**Bell.** An ancient Eastern symbol used by the
priests to summon the Supreme Spirit. Bells were
believed to have the power of subduing storms and
driving away plagues and demons. Hence the bell
is one of the symbols of St. Anthony. The bull
Nandi the *nahan* of Siva was always depicted with a
bell hanging by a cord or chain around the neck. The
ancients often decorated the handle with a flaring
three-fold top either three circles, the trefoil or the
*fleur-de-lys*. Sometimes the handle was the *vajra* or
thunderbolt. The Buddhists attached a similar meaning to the *vajra* and the bell to that of the *linga* and
*yoni* of the Hindus. The *vajra* represented Buddha,
the creative principle, the *linga*, and the bell Dharma,
matter, the feminine principle, the *yoni*. The bell was
an old symbol of virginity. The bell was looked upon
by the early Christians not only as the "call of Christ
but as a sign of Christ Himself." The custom of
tolling a bell to announce a death, the number of
strokes representing the age of the deceased persisted
for ages. Durandus in the *Symbolism of Churches*
says, "Moreover the bells ought to be rung when
anyone is dying that the people hearing this may
pray for him. For a woman indeed they ring twice,
because she first caused the bitterness of death; for
she first alienated mankind from God, wherefore the

second day had no benediction. But for a man they ring three times, because the Trinity was first shown in man." Durandus was born about the year 1220 A.D. when the feminine principle was still somewhat in disrepute.

**Bes.** One of the oldest Egyptian gods and called by Churchward a primary form of Horus I. Other authorities identify Bes with Set or Typhon. Budge says, "The figure of this god suggests that his home was a place where the dwarf and pigmy were held in high esteem. . . . The knowledge of the god and perhaps figures of him were brought from this region which the Egyptians called the 'Land of the Spirits.' " According to another legend Bes was a foreigner introduced into Egypt from the land of Punt (the spice land of Arabia). In some aspects he resembles Bacchus and presides over gaiety, music, dancing. As a war god he carries a sword. Representations of him are hideous and grotesque. He is depicted as a squat, crooked dwarf sometimes wearing an animal's skin with the tail hanging down behind. His tongue is frequently extended and often he has a crown of feathers. His sacred animal was the sow. There is a small temple to Bes at Denderah. On one of the royal chariots found in the tomb of Tut-ankh-amen the straps of the harness saddle of the breast harness pass through the mouth of the god Bes.

**Black.** In China and Japan black was associated with the north, *yin* and water.

**Blue.** The Egyptians, also Swedenborg, made blue the symbol of Truth. Blue is the symbol of the feminine principle, signifying also heaven, fidelity, constancy. In Christian art Christ and the Divine Mother wear the blue mantle typifying heavenly love and heavenly truth. St. John the Evangelist was given the blue tunic and the red mantle.

**Buddha.** He is said to have been born eleven times as a deer and to have preached his first sermon in a deer park. Thus a gilded wheel between two gazelles or deer found in Buddhist temples symbolises the preaching of Buddha. Other symbols are the circle, swastika, lotus, ûrnâ—the precious gem usually a moon stone or flaming pearl worn on the forehead between the eyes. [See Ûrnâ.] Statues of Buddha represent him in many postures, standing, seated with legs crossed, or recumbent.

**Buddha's Eight Familiar Symbols.** Also called the "eight lucky emblems." The conch, umbrella, canopy, knot, fish, lotus, jar and wheel of the law.

**Buddhist Symbols.** Rope, axe, goad or spear, scroll of texts, begging bowl, sacrificial cup, fan, bow and arrow, wheel, incense burner, rosary, lotus, fly brush, hare and moon, cock and the sun, the vase for shrine use, musical instruments and calabash or medicine bottle.

**Builder's Square.** Used symbolically in the Egyp-

tian ritual, also represented in temples and the Great
Pyramid as seats for Osiris and Maat, the goddess of
Truth. In the judgment hall Osiris is seated on the
Square. This is also a Masonic emblem.

**Bull-roarer.** One of the most ancient and widespread religious symbols in the world resembling the
rhombus which figured in the ancient mysteries of
Greece. It consists of a slab of wood tied to a piece
of string which upon being whirled rapidly round
gives forth an unearthly, roaring sound. It was used,
it is presumed, as a sacred instrument to evoke the
Supreme Spirit who manifested himself in the blasts of
the mighty wind. It is still used by the Australians
and New Zealanders and is also employed in their
religious ceremonies by the natives of Africa, Ceylon
and the Malay Peninsula.

**Burning Lamps.** At Sais a great feature of the
annual commemoration of the death of Osiris was
that of lighted lamps filled with oil which were kept
burning day and night till the festival was over. The
same custom of lighting the souls of the dead on All
Soul's day was observed in other places. In Japan
it is called the Feast of Lanterns.

**Calabash or Gourd** typified the creative power of
nature. The Chinese placed it on a tripod as a
symbol of blessing and fertility. Druggists kept
medicines in gourd-shaped bottles. For the same
reason the Elixir of Life was stored in a calabash.

**Canopic Jars.** A name given to the vases used by the Egyptians for the viscera which were removed from the body in the process of mummification and treated separately. The jars, four in number were placed near the sarcophagus and were under the special protection of the four gods of the dead, the sons of Horus Hapi, Amset, Duamutef and Kebeh-senuf who were represented respectively with the head of a baboon, man, jackal and hawk. After the xviii dynasty it was customary to put the symbolic heads of these gods on the covers of the jars.

**Canopy.** A symbol of sovereignty and carried over the heads of Eastern rulers and emperors on state occasions. When placed over the head of Buddha its shelter typified the sacred tree under which he received enlightenment.

**Cantharus.** A two-handled Greek vase or cup sacred to Dionysos who is frequently represented holding it in his hand.

**Cap with Up-turned Horns.** A symbol among the Babylonians of divine power. A cap or turban on a seat or altar may have been used to typify the "world mountain," the symbol of the chief Babylonian triad Anu, Enlil and Ea.

**Castor and Pollux.** [See Dioscuri.]

**Ceres.** [See Demeter.]

**Chains.** "That excellent and Divine fable of the Golden Chain, namely, that Men were not able to draw Jupiter down to earth; but contrariwise Jupiter was able to draw them up to Heaven." [Bacon.]

**Cherub.** The head of an angel emerging from two wings and used as an ornament in sculpture and painting.

**Cherubim.** A term derived from the Assyrian and now used to signify angels or those of the second degree of the nine-fold celestial hierarchy who have the gift of knowledge as the first (the seraphim) have the gift of love. The cherubim in the temple of Jerusalem and Solomon's Palace have been identified with the winged bull of Assyria; from these also came the winged figures that modern art received at the hands of the Greeks. The bird power, associated with the deity by the Egyptians and Assyrians, was humanised by the Greeks in their flying angels of victory.

**Chimera.** A fabulous, fire-breathing monster with three heads, that of a dragon, a goat and a lion. Homer described it as having the head of a lion, body of a goat and tail of a dragon. It was Bellerophon who, mounted on his winged horse Pegasus succeeded in destroying it. The chimera is frequently represented on ancient Greek coins and various combinations of fantastic animals called chimeræ were used in the Middle Ages as caryatids or supports in pieces of furniture. The term chimerical applied to anything without semblance of truth or reality is derived from the chimera.

**Cinquecento.** An abbreviation for *mille cinquecento* and applied to the art of Italy in the 16th century.

**Cista.** The mystic *cist* or chest in which were kept the articles that pertained to the worship of Demeter and Dionysos and belonging to the same class of images as the ark of the Egyptians and the Jews.

**Clover Leaf (St. Patrick's Shamrock).** An emblem of the Deity more ancient than Christianity. As the gods were worshipped in triads and the three-fold aspect of life recognised in all its significance the trefoil became a natural emblem of high importance and a widely accepted symbol of the Trinity.

**Compass.** Among the ancient Chinese the compass and square were used as symbols of right conduct as in the masonic orders of to-day.

**Conch-shell.** A symbol of the voice of Buddha or the preaching of Buddha. It is one of the eight familiar symbols of Buddha and also typifies the *yoni* or feminine principle.

**Criophorus.** A Greek word which means literally "one who carries a ram." It was a name bestowed upon Hermes by the people of Tanagra because he had saved them from a plague by carrying a ram (thrice?) around the walls of the town. Hermes is frequently represented thus in Greek art.

**Cupid.** [See Eros.]

**Demeter (Ceres).** The Greek goddess of the earth, daughter of Kronos and Rhea and mother of Perse-

phone and Dionysos by Zeus. Aided by Zeus, Pluto
carries off Persephone to the lower world. The rape
of Persephone and the anger of the goddess mother
which results in a famine on earth when nothing is
permitted to grow is simply another embodiment of
the old nature myth of the winter season when the
productive powers of nature or the earth rest or lie
concealed. Zeus yielding to her entreaties permits
Persephone to spend half the year with her mother
and Persephone in whose charge the seed is committed
to the earth typified the "fructified flower that returns
in the spring" dwelling in the light a portion of the
year. Worship of Demeter has been connected with
belief in a future life and the Eleusinian mysteries
celebrated in her honour were said to have had an
ennobling effect. Demeter not only was goddess of
the fertility of the earth but of fertility in general
and thus was the goddess of marriage. She was worshipped in Attica, Crete, Delos, Sicily and the west
coast of Asia. She is the goddess of agriculture, of
corn and harvests. Pigs, symbols of fertility were
sacrificed to her, also cows, bulls, honey cakes and
fruits. In art the goddess is represented draped
and with a veil. She frequently wears a garland
of ears of corn, in her hand she holds a sceptre,
an ear of corn or a poppy and sometimes a torch and
the mystic basket. Her expression is one of great
dignity.

THE YOUTHFUL BACCHUS
(Museo Nazionale, Naples.)

Photo, Alinari

**DIONYSOS**
(Museo Nazionale, Naples.)

**Diana.**  [See Artemis.]

**Dionysos (Bacchus).**    The god of the vintage and
the cultivation of the earth was called both by the
Greeks and the Romans "Bacchus, the noisy or riot-
ous god." This was originally, however, merely a
surname for Dionysos.  The legends of this god are
innumerable, his adventures endless.  He was said
to be a son of Zeus by Semele, he was also called the
son of Zeus and Leto, Zeus and Persephone, Zeus and
Demeter as well as many others.  The father never
varies nor do any of the legends minimise the wrath
of the jealous Hera.  Zeus was said to have placed
him in his thigh and given him to the nymphs of
Mount Nysa who brought him up.  He was also
associated with the Muses and Hermes is some-
how mixed up with the early life of the god who is
frequently represented as a child carried by Hermes.
Dionysos is said to have discovered the cultivation
of the vine and wanders over various countries of the
earth teaching its uses.  One legend tells of his coming to a lake and one of two asses whom he met on
the shore carried him safely across.  The god placed
both animals among the stars and henceforth the
ass was sacred to Dionysos.  His influence is both
benign and evil.  He is god of the "productive, over-
flowing and intoxicating power of nature which carries man away from his usual quiet and sober mode
of living."  As god of wine he is inspired as well as

inspiring and thus has the power of prophecy. He is also a god of healing and as protector of the vine, he becomes protector of trees and thus comes into close relationship with Demeter. Like Apollo he was thought to possess eternal youth. In the earlier period the Graces or Charites were his companions. In later times he was worshipped as androgynous. Afterwards, as his worship changed he was accompanied by bacchantes, wild and dishevelled women, satyrs and centaurs inspired with divine fury and carrying in their hands thyrsus staffs, cymbals, swords and serpents. Dionysos is a twice-born god of vegetation, a promoter of civilisation and lover of peace. He is also god of the drama and protector of theatres. He is depicted in art as an infant with Hermes or being played with by satyrs. As the youthful or Theban Bacchus his body is masculine with firm outlines but with a certain softness and roundness which suggests the feminine. His expression is dreamy and languid, the head is crowned by a diadem or wreath of vine leaves or ivy. He is frequently depicted leaning on his comrades, or riding on an ass, lion, tiger or panther. Occasionally, on coins only, he is given the horns of a ram or bull. His attributes are the thyrsus, cantharus or drinking cup and sometimes the basket. The vine, asphodel, laurel, ivy, panther, ass, serpent, tiger and lynx were sacred to him. The ox and ram were sacrificed to

him. Dionysos was said to have "loathed the sight
of an owl."

**The Dioscuri (Castor and Pollux).** The twin
horsemen, one mortal the other immortal, represent
the setting and rising sun. In Egypt they were
called the Two Lions, Yesterday and To-day. In
India they were called *Vitrahana* because they ushered
in the Sunlight and destroyed Vritra, the Darkness.
They are the Açwins, the special gods of horsemen
and are given white horses. They are also symbolised
by twin circles.

**Dorjé.** A small sceptre used by the lamas of Tibet
composed of two or four tridents combined, the outer
prongs touching the central one giving the whole
something the appearance of a crown.

**Egg.** In one of the Hindu creation myths the
Supreme Spirit laid a golden egg resplendent as the
sun. From this was born Brahma the progenitor of
the universe. Egypt had the Chaos Goose who
cackled loudly to the Chaos Gander when she laid
the egg of the sun. The Cosmic egg, 'the germ of the
universe' occurs in many mythologies with or without
the 'precious goose.' Bayley suggests that the fairy
tale of the goose that laid the golden egg may have
been derived from this ancient myth. [1]

**Eight.** The figure 8 typified regeneration. It is
one of the symbols of the Egyptian god Thoth who

[1] Bayley's *Lost Language of Symbolism.*

"pours the waters of purification on the heads of the initiated." Swedenborg makes eight correspond to purification.

**Eros (Cupid).** The god of love. Hesiod, the earliest author that mentions him describes him as the cosmogonic Eros. "First . . . there was Chaos, then came Ge, Tartarus and Eros, the fairest among the gods, who rules over the minds and councils of gods and men. . . . Eros was one of the fundamental causes in the formation of the world, inasmuch as he was the uniting power of love which brought order and harmony among the conflicting elements of which Chaos consisted." In accordance with this conception he was called a son of Kronos or a god who came into existence without parentage. It is only among the later poets that he is represented as a wanton boy, sometimes as the son of Aphrodite, sometimes the son of Hermes and Artemis, or again he is given a mother but not a father. In this later aspect he typified the love of the senses which begets disharmony rather than unity. He makes sport of gods and men. He twists the thunderbolts of Zeus, tames lions and takes away his arms from Herakles. He was given a bow and arrows which he carried in a golden quiver, some golden and others blunt and heavy as lead. He has golden wings and is frequently represented blindfolded. He is often depicted with Aphrodite also with Hermes and statues of Hermes

and Eros usually stood in the Greek gymnasia.
Thespiæ in Bœotia was the chief place of the worship
of Eros and where in ancient days he was represented
by a rude stone. He was also worshipped in Samos,
Sparta and Athens. He was a favourite subject with
the Greek sculptors. Praxiteles, who represented him
as a full grown youth of great beauty being especially
famed for his statues of the god of love. Later the
fashion grew to depict him as a winged infant or
wanton child. He is thus shown in the illustration of
*Ares in Repose*. Wild beasts are sometimes shown
tamed by the god. His attributes are the ram, hare,
cock and rose.

**Eye.** A symbol of Horus and Osiris typifying
divine omniscience. The same meaning is also attached to it in India. According to St. Matthew the
single eye symbolises light. "The light of the body
is the eye; if therefore thine eye be single thy whole
body shall be full of light." (Matt. 6 : 22.)

**Fan.** An ancient Chinese emblem of power and
dominion.

**Feather.** An attribute of Maat the Egyptian goddess of Truth.

**Foot-prints of Buddha.** There are usually seven
emblems on the soles of the feet, the swastika, wheel,
conch-shell, fish, vajra, crown, vase. The idea was
taken over from Vishnu, an earlier god.

**Ganesha.** An Indian god who is invoked by the

Hindus as an overcomer of obstacles. He is represented by an elephant or a man with the head of an
elephant. Images of Ganesha are found at cross
roads and architects place figures of the god at the
foundation of buildings.

**Gazelle.** An animal sacred to Mul-lil, the Akkadian
god of storms who was originally the lord (mul) of
the dust (lil), that is, the husband of the earth, the
phallic father or great snake. The oryx, goat (wild
goat or ibex), and the antelope are all the equivalents
of the gazelle and are all typhonic, symbols of Set.
Horus tramples under foot the gazelle. Horus holding a gazelle typifies his victory over Set. Lunar
crescents are associated with gazelles. The association of deer, the ibex or wild goat, oryx, gazelle or
antelope with the lotus is symbolic of the sun or moon
or both. Deer are given to Diana. The Hindu moon
god Chandra rides in a car drawn by antelopes. An
antelope is given to Siva who is represented by a
moon crescent.

**Girdle Tie in Red Carnelian.** An Egyptian amulet
typifying the blood of Isis and which had the power
to wash away the sins of its possessor.

**Gorgons, The.** There were three gorgons with
"curls of hissing snakes" instead of hair and whoever
gazed upon them was turned to stone. All were
immortal except Medusa, whom Perseus encouraged
by Athene succeeds in killing and her head was worn

henceforth upon the ægis of Athene. Medusa was frequently represented in Greek art. The head seen full face with serpents coiled about it, the face one of horror with parted lips was much used for decorative purposes. Small images of the head of Medusa were also used as charms.

**Griffin, Griffon, Gryphon.** Fabulous creatures, half-lion, half-eagle symbolising eternal vigilance and wardenship. They were the protectors of the treasured gold of the North from the thieving, one-eyed Arimaspians and are also mentioned as guarding the gold of India.

**Grove.** Often a mis-translation for the wooden image of Ashtoreth or Astarte the chief goddess of Baalism.

**Hathor.** The Egyptian goddess of the feminine principle in nature. As goddess of maternity she is given the head of a vulture surmounted by the moon crescent or horns and the solar disk. Again she is represented as the World Cow typifying fertility. "The heads of Hathor were lucky charms. Hathor represented fate, and he who wore her head earned her favour and a happy destiny for himself." She is a cosmic goddess, the mother of light and sometimes represented as a sphinx.

**Hephæstos (Vulcan).** In early Greek art the god of fire is depicted as a dwarfish figure in allusion to his lameness. In the finest period of Greek art he is represented as a full-bearded man of powerful frame.

He wears an oval cap and the *chiton* leaving the right arm and shoulder bare. His symbol is the hammer and sometimes he is given the tongs.

**Hera (Juno).** The "only really married goddess among the Olympians" and one of the few divinities who are purely Greek. Unlike the other great nature goddesses Hera was not the "Queen of gods and men" but the wife of the Supreme god Zeus and equally reverenced by the other gods. Zeus listens to her counsels and she feels free to censure him when occasion offers. Nevertheless, she is his inferior in power and obliged to obey him. She is represented as obstinate, jealous, quarrelsome and quite ready to resort to cunning and intrigue to compass her ends. Hera personifies the atmosphere, she is "Queen of the Air," the great goddess of nature and is identified with the Roman Juno. Her most celebrated temple was at Mt. Embœa. A colossal sitting statue of Hera of gold and ivory made for her sanctuary was the work of Polycletus. She was often depicted wearing a crown adorned with the Charites and Horæ and holding in one hand a pomegranate and in the other a sceptre surmounted by a cuckoo. She was frequently represented veiled. In the earliest form of her worship the goddess was represented by a pillar or possibly the "aniconic image" that was associated with most of the great nature goddesses. The peacock and cuckoo were sacred to her.

HATHOR. XVIII–XIX DYNASTY
(Carnarvon Collection, Metropolitan
Museum of Art.)

ISIS-HATHOR. XXI–XXIII DYNASTY (1090–718 B.C.)
(Carnarvon Collection, Metropolitan Museum of Art.)

THOUERIS (TA-URT), ONE
OF THE OLDEST MOTHER
GODDESSES, HOLDING
SYMBOL OF ISIS.
P T O L E M A I C
PERIOD (332–
30 B.C.)
(Carnarvon Collection,
Metropolitan Museum
of Art.)

GODDESS SEXHMET,
KARNAK
(Metropolitan Museum
of Art.)

**Herakles.** The most celebrated hero of antiquity and a son of Zeus by Alcmene of Thebes, wife of Amphitryon. His birth arouses the jealous wrath of Hera who sends two snakes to devour him before he was eight months old. The infant Herakles seizes them and crushes them in both his hands. His first great victory was his fight with the lion of Cythæron. Henceforth Herakles wore the lion's skin as his ordinary garment with its head for a helmet. Some accounts give him the lion's skin as an attribute of his victory over the Nemean lion. The subservience of Herakles to Eurystheus was brought about by the strategy of Hera. Zeus having decreed that the one who came into the world last must obey the other has to stand by his word. He makes Hera promise, however, that if Herakles performs twelve great works in the service of Eurystheus he shall become immortal. The latter imposes upon him many and bitter tasks. The Twelve Labours of Herakles are: (1) The fight with the lion of Nemea which Herakles strangled with his own hands. (2) To destroy the Lernean hydra, a monster with nine heads, the middle one immortal. (3) To bring alive and unhurt to Eurystheus, the stag of Ceryneia in Arcadia, famous for its incredible swiftness, its golden horns and brazen feet and sacred to Artemis. (4) To bring alive to Eurystheus the wild boar which ravaged the Erymanthian neighbourhood. On this adventure he destroyed the

centaurs.   (5) The fifth labour was to clean the
Augean stables where 3000 oxen had been kept for
many years.   (6) To kill the Stymphalian birds which
infested a lake in Arcadia and fed on human flesh.
(7) To bring alive into Peloponnesus the Cretan wild
bull.   (8) To capture the mares of the Thracian
Diomedes that tore and devoured human flesh.   (9)
To obtain the girdle of the queen of the Amazons.
(10) To destroy the monster Geryones and bring his
oxen alive to Argos.  It was upon this expedition that
Herakles erected the two pillars (Calpe and Abyla)
on the two sides of the straits of Gibraltar which were
thereafter called the Pillars of Herakles.   On this
journey, too, Herakles, enraged by the heat of the
sun shot at Helios who, admiring his boldness, presented him with a golden boat in which he sailed
across the ocean to Erytheia.   (11) The eleventh
labour was to obtain the golden apples from the
garden of the Hesperides.  It was upon this adventure
that Herakles killed the vulture that was consuming
the liver of Prometheus and thus saved the Titan,
who in return advised him not to go to the garden of
the Hesperides but to send Atlas and in the mean-
time to bear the weight of heaven for Atlas on his
own shoulders.   Atlas having brought the apples
refused to take upon himself again the burden of
heaven and declared his intention of carrying the
apples to Eurystheus.  In this case Herakles employed

strategy to obtain the apples and accomplish his mission. (12) The last and most dangerous of his labours was to bring upon earth from the lower world the three-headed dog Cerberus. Having successfully performed these twelve feats of heroism, his life is still one of vicissitude. In the end having been unwittingly poisoned by his wife, leaving him with an incurable distemper Herakles climbs Mount Œta and imploring the protection of Zeus he raises a pile of wood which he mounts and orders to be set on fire. None of his followers would obey him. Finally a shepherd passing by complies and while the pyre is burning a cloud comes down from heaven and amid peals of thunder Zeus bears the hero to Olympus where he becomes one of the immortals. After the apotheosis of Herakles, sacrifices were offered to him as a hero. Later on he was worshipped throughout Greece as a divinity. Herakles, Pan and Dionysos were called the youngest gods. The worship of Herakles spread to Rome and Italy and from there into Gaul, Spain and Germany. The Roman Hercules was looked upon as the giver of health. Representations of Herakles in art cover every phase of his life. Whether depicted as youth, hero or immortal he is always the type of unconquerable strength, energy and resourcefulness. His labours are undertaken for the good of others, never for himself. He is also called a solar god and his twelve labours represent the twelve signs of the zodiac. He is usually depicted wearing the lion's skin or with it over one arm. The animals sacrificed to him were the bull, ram, lamb and boar.

**Hermes (Mercury).** He is the god of prudence, commerce, eloquence, skill, of cunning and strategy; he is a thieving god, one who would steal or commit fraud or perjury without a qualm, accomplishing his ends with invincible dexterity and gracefulness. He was the herald and messenger of the gods. In his ministry to Zeus not only was he a herald but also the charioteer and cup bearer. He was said to have been the inventor of the alphabet, numbers, astronomy, gymnastics, the art of warfare and the cultivation of the olive tree. It was Hermes who invented the lyre which he bestowed upon Apollo, receiving in exchange the caduceus. As dreams are sent by Zeus, Hermes conducts them to man and thus he has the power of giving or taking away sleep. He was god of the roads and the protector of travellers. He was the giver of wealth and good luck and thus was the god of gamblers. As the protector of animals he was especially worshipped by shepherds. In the Arcadian religion Hermes was the fertilising god of the earth. One of his most important functions was that of conducting the souls of the dead from the upper to the lower regions. As conductor of the dead he always carries the caduceus with the two emblematic serpents,

symbols of life. In the earlier works of art Hermes
was depicted with a ram over his shoulder. He was
then called Hermes Criophorus. [See Criophorus.]
In this aspect he becomes the prototype of Christ as
the Shepherd. His usual attributes are the *petasos*—
a low wide-rimmed hat sometimes adorned with little
wings—winged sandals to denote the swiftness with
which he could girdle the universe, the magic staff
later developed into the caduceus, and sometimes as
god of wealth he holds a purse in his hand. The palm,
tortoise, cock, ram, goat, various kinds of fish and
the number four were sacred to him. Incense, cakes
and honey, lambs, young goats and pigs were sacrificial offerings.

**Herms or Hermæ.** Statues of Hermes, the god of
ways, were placed at street corners, cross roads and
boundaries. The statues of the phallic Hermes used
as boundary stones were often in the form of a cross
with pointed heads. Those placed at three road
junctions were called *Trivia*. The name Hermæ is
given to a peculiar kind of statue consisting of a carefully modelled head or bust set upon a quadrangular
pillar tapering toward the base. Sometimes there is
a single head or again a double head is set on the
pillar. This form of statue is of great antiquity
and was highly honoured. To deface the Hermæ
was looked upon as a serious crime. The Romans
used the Hermæ in the decoration of gardens or as

pillars set at intervals in balustrades or walls. Later, terminal figures of bearded gods or even philosophers were also called Hermæ.

**Horus.** Prince of Eternity. "I am yesterday, to-day and to-morrow." Horus is the morning sun, the type of eternal youth. He is given the hawk, sometimes represented as a falcon or hawk. He wears a double diadem as ruler over the North and South. Originally one of the oldest gods of Egypt he returns as the son of Osiris and Isis.

**Incense.** Priests burned incense in Egypt to smoke out demons and drive out evil spirits. It was believed also to aid the soul in its last flight. Inspiration was derived from it. The gods were invoked and propitiated by it. In the flood legend the Babylonian Noah burned incense. It is used wherever there is Buddhism as in the Catholic religion of to-day.

**Incense Burners.** When made in the form of lions indicate the association of the lion with fire and sun worship. The lion is thus the god and producer of smoke.

**Indra.** The Hindu god who makes rain. Indra is called the god of 10,000 eyes, or Lord and Watcher of the Stars. His symbol is the *vajra* or thunderbolt.

**Isis.** She is usually depicted in the form of a woman with the vulture headdress and holding the papyrus sceptre, or again with the solar disk resting in the crescent horns above her head, and sometimes she wears the double crown of North and South. She has the uræus snake on her forehead, is given the lotus and all the sacred animals. Her peculiar attribute is the Sistrum. [See Sistrum.]

**Ivy.** Denoted eternal life, hence placed upon the brow of Bacchus.

**Jade.** In China it symbolises "all that is supremely excellent," the highest form of human virtue, the "most perfect development of the masculine principle in nature."

**Janus.** A god who rivalled Jupiter himself among the Romans. Janus releases the dawn, he is also the god of the beginning and end of undertakings. He is represented in art as two-faced and is given the key as a symbol of his power to open and close. In time of war his temple in Rome was open, and closed in times of peace.

**Jug.** One of the eight familiar symbols of Buddha. It gives forth no sound when full, typifying a man full of knowledge.

**Juno.** [See Hera.]

**Jupiter.** [See Zeus.]

**Ka.** This is man's double, a replica of the body but formed of a substance less dense—"an etherealised projection of the individual." The Egyptians pictured the Ka as the vital force which came into the world with the body, passed through life in its company and went with it into the next world. Everything in Egypt was supposed to have a double.

**Kalasa.** The Vase which holds the Water of Life. A symbol of the Chinese goddess Kwan-yin.

**Keys.** Symbol of Janus who flings wide open the portals of the sky and releases the Dawn. Also given to Mithra, the Persian sun-god, and to St. Peter, prince of the apostles and founder of the Church of Rome.

**Knot.** Without beginning or end, the mystic sign of Vishnu, typifying the continuity of life and adopted by the Buddhists as one of the eight glorious emblems of Buddha.

**Kwan-yin.** In spite of their philosophy which recognised that displacement, continual displacement rather than ultimate balance and union is the law of the universe, and that Life is not a mould but a living, changing thing, the Chinese yielded to the hunger for union in their goddess Kwan-yin (the Japanese Kwan-non), the feminine form of the god of mercy, Avalokitésvara, and worshipped as both masculine and feminine. Regarded as masculine by the priests and educated classes, the feminine form was more generally favoured both in China and Japan. To the common people Kwan-yin is the goddess of infinite mercy and compassion. "She of a thousand arms." She is depicted in Buddhist art seated upon a lotus and again with many arms. She is frequently shown holding the *Kalasa* or with it at her side. A willow branch with which she sprinkles the Waters of Life is either in the sacred vase or she holds it in her hand. The masculine form of Kwan-yin is often shown with the lotus bud in the *Kalaśa*.

**Labarum.** The famous labarum of Constantine, according to Bayley was used long before Christianity and "probably stood for X the Great Fire and P, *pater* or *Patah*." Other scholars look upon it as an adaptation of the solar wheel. It has many forms.

VARIOUS FORMS OF CONSTANTINE'S MONOGRAM OR CROSS.

**Ladder.** A favourite symbol of the ascent to the gods. The ladder of Jacob was probably derived from the Egyptian belief that you could mount to heaven on a ladder. Small ladders as amulets were placed in the tombs of Egyptian kings.

Sakya-muni was said to have descended from the Tushita heaven by a ladder brought to him by Indra. This ladder is often portrayed with the footprints of Buddha on the top and bottom rung.

In the mysteries of Mithra a ladder of seven steps

composed of seven different kinds of metal representing the seven spheres of the planets by means of which souls ascended and descended, symbolised the passage of the soul. The superstition that walking under a ladder brings bad luck may be a relic of this ancient superstition, typifying the sinister side, the refusal to climb, one who dodges, ignores the true way to salvation.

**Lightning.** Symbolised in all nations by a weapon. Thunder and storm gods were given the axe, hammer, pitchfork, trident, the *vajra* or thunderbolt. Sometimes a trident with zigzag branches was used to typify forked lightning.

**Lituus.** A twisted wand something like a bishop's crosier and used by augurs for purposes of divination. When depicted in art it usually takes the form of a spiral.

**Lizard.** A giant lizard was a symbol of Ahrimanes, the Persian god of evil. A lizard is occasionally depicted upon the breast of Athene. It was thought to conceive through the ear and bring forth through the mouth and was worshipped in Mexico and by the Slav nations as late as the sixteenth century.

**Love.** According to Greek mythology Love issued from the egg of night floating on Chaos. Ouspensky calls "love a symbol of equilibrium and the road to Infinity." Love has been compared to a fire giving warmth; intelligence to a light-giving flame.

**Mars.**  [See Ares.]

**Medusa.**  [See Gorgons.]

**Menat, or Whip Amulet.**  Symbolic of strength and supposed to drive away care.  The menat is the handle of the whip which was used to keep off evil spirits and as an amulet was frequently surmounted by the head of a goddess.  It is also a symbol of pleasure and happiness.

**Mercury.**  [See Hermes.]

**Minerva.**  [See Athene.]

**Mirror.**  One of the symbols of truth.  The mirror of self-realisation, the shield which evil dare not face. Concave bronze mirrors are conspicuous among the Taoist symbols, the belief being that "when evil recognises itself it destroys itself."  Mirrors were also thought to ward off evil spirits.

**Mouse.**  Sacred to Apollo.  "Cinderella's coach was drawn by *mice* which turned magically into white horses, i.e., the golden footed steeds of the Morning."  (Bayley.)

**Mut.**  The feminine counterpart of Amen-Ra, the great "world Mother."  She is represented as a woman wearing the united crowns of North and South and holding in one hand the *ankh* cross and in the other the papyrus sceptre.  Sometimes she has large wings and at her feet is the feather symbol of Maat.  Again from each shoulder there projects the head of a vulture.  Sometimes she has the head of a man or a woman or a vulture or lioness. When given the phallus and the head of a man it denoted the belief that the goddess was androgynous, or self-produced.

**Nephthys.** Sister of Isis and wife of Set, typified death, corruption, diminution, sterility. Although goddess of death she symbolised the coming into existence of the life which springs from death. She is represented as a woman with a pair of horns and the disk.

**Neptune.** [See Poseidon.]

**Numbers.** Plato assigned dexter things and odd numbers to the Olympic gods and the opposite to the dæmons. The Pythagoreans used the unit and odd numbers for good, and the even numbers for whatever is fluent, crooked, indeterminate, evil.

Among the Pythagoreans:—

*1—is the number of essence.*

*2—signified otherness, involving difference, diversity.*

*3—mediation, atonement, completeness—beginning, middle, end.*

*4—indicated squareness, justice, earth.*

*5—being the combination of odd and even symbolised marriage.*

*6—the number of luck or chance.*

*7—was the number of the entire cosmos, 3 representing the deity and 4 the world. God and the world.*

*8—solidity.*

*9—the treble triad.  The cube of three being nine,*
*nine was regarded by Pythagoras as the extent*
*to which numbers would go, all others being*
*embraced and revolving within it.  Ten but*
*recommences a fresh series capable of infinite*
*expansion.*

"At Babylon a number was a very different thing
from a *figure*.  Just as in ancient times and above all
in Egypt, the *name* had a magic power, and ceremonial
words formed an irresistible incantation, so here the
number possesses an active force, the number is a
symbol, and its properties are sacred attributes." [1]

We have seen that **Three** was a supremely sacred
number, also **Eight** and **Nine**.  Then, too, the revolving year with its recurring seasons, marked into
twelve periods of time or months by the new moon,
the twelve hours between sunrise and sunset,—the
Chinese as well as the Babylonians divided the day
of twenty-four hours into double hours believing that
it bore a definite relationship to the twelve signs of
the zodiac and the twelve mansions of the elliptic—
the four cardinal points, the four seasons, the seven
days of the week made the numbers 4, 7 and 12 for
thousands of years sacred numbers of highest
significance.

The Four Ages were originally the four seasons

[1] Cumont's *Astrology and Religion*, p. 30.

The sun-god was associated with the Spring—the Italian *primavera* is a most lovely and expressive word for the season that brings to view once more the association of the mighty sun with the re-awakening of nature. The moon belonged to the summer, Venus presided over the autumn months and Mars was the god of winter. The Greeks, however, gave to their Aphrodite (Venus), goddess of love and beauty the month of April—*aperilis*—the opening, the germinating month.

The sun, moon and five planets become the "sacred seven." The five planets like sun and moon "traversed the constellations of the zodiac," and in Babylonia were identified with the great deities. "Jupiter whose golden light burns most steadily in the sky" was assigned to Marduk, Venus was one of the forms of the goddess Ishtar, Saturn fell to Ninib, Mercury to Nebo and Mars to Nergal, the god of war.

The seven days of the week belong to the "sacred seven." Sunday is the day of Mithra the sun-god. Monday (Ital. *lunedi*, Fr. *lundi*) belongs to Diana the moon-goddess. Tuesday (Ital. *martedi*, Fr. *mardi*) is the day of Mars. Wednesday (Ital. *mercoledi*, Fr. *mercredi*) belongs to Mercury. Thursday (Ital. *giovedi*, Fr. *jeudi*) to Jupiter (Jove), the Teutonic Thor. Friday (Ital. *venerdi*, Fr. *vendredi*) to Venus. Friday also corresponds to the German *Freitag* the day of

Fria or Freya the Teutonic goddess of love. Saturday
(Ital. *sabato*, Fr. *samedi*) is the day of Saturn.

These planets were the tutelary deities, not alone of
the days but of the hours, years, centuries and even
the thousand of years. To each planet was ascribed
a plant, a stone and a metal. These derived peculiar
and miraculous powers under this benign and celestial
protection.

The Babylonians gave the following colours to the
sun, moon and five planets:—The Sun, gold; the
Moon, silver; Jupiter, orange; Venus, yellow; Saturn,
black; Mars, red; and Mercury, blue.

"The magic idea of a power superior to man was
connected from the very beginning with the notation
of time." [1]

Infinity of time was exalted as the Supreme
Cause.

Sacred calendars regulated religious ceremonies and
civil life according to the course of the moon. These
calendars were of high religious import in star worship,
their most important function being to record the
days and hours or periods of time which would be
auspicious or inauspicious.

Among the Mithraites Time was represented as a
huge monster with the head of a lion to show that he
devours all things. Again Time is shown helping
Truth out of a cave.

[1] *Astrology and Religion*, Franz Cumont, p. 108.

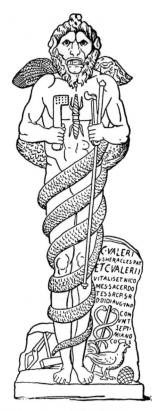

**LION-HEADED FIGURE OF THE MITHRAIC KRONOS OR BOUND-LESS TIME.**

The body is entwined six times by a serpent, and four wings having the symbols of the four seasons spring from the back. A thunderbolt is engraved on the breast. In the left hand is a key and in the right a key and sceptre or long rod the emblem of authority. At the foot of the statue are the hammer and tongs of Vulcan, the cock, the sacred cone and the wand of Mercury typifying that the power of all the gods is embodied in the Mithraic Suturn.

Cumont, *Mysteries of Mithra.*

Numbers were held sacred, but unlike Time and all its divisions were never deified.

**Orpheus.** He is said by some to be a son of Apollo and has been called the inventor of letters and everything that pertains to civilisation. Receiving a lyre from Apollo he charmed the beasts and birds by the magic of his music. Rivers ceased to flow in order to hear him and mountains moved nearer to listen to his song. His love for Eurydice is founded on the old nature myth of death and restoration to life. Upon the death of Eurydice, Orpheus descends to the nether regions searching for her and gains the consent of Pluto that she shall be restored to life and free to accompany him back to earth, if he will refrain from looking at her until after they are beyond the precincts of hell. When in sight of the upper region of light Orpheus turned to gaze upon her and Eurydice melted from his sight. Mourning for his lost love he withdrew into himself. The Thracian women angered by his coldness tore him limb from limb and threw his head in the Hebrus. Orpheus was called the first poet of the Heroic Age. The Orphics were a mystic order founded upon the doctrines and teachings of Orpheus. In early Christian art Christ was depicted as Orpheus surrounded by beasts and birds whom He charmed by His music.

**Osiris.** His symbols are the **Eye** and the **Sceptre** typifying providence and power. He has the head of a hawk or a man, and holds the *crux ansata* in his hand. As god of the dead he wears the Atef crown with plumes, and in his hands are the **Crook, Sceptre and Flail,** symbols of rule, sovereignty and dominion. Osiris is usually depicted in mummy form wearing the White Crown and a *menat* hanging from the back of his neck and holding the crook, sceptre and flail. Sometimes he wears the Atef, the white crown with plumes, sometimes he appears in the form of the tet (tat) pillar.

**Osiris, his Amulets.**   The amulets used in producing the reconstitution of the body of Osiris, torn asunder by Set, were: the four figures of the children of Horus, two bulls, a figure of Horus, four lapis-lazuli tat pillars, two carnelian tat pillars, a figure of Thoth, and two lapis-lazuli *uzats*.

**Pan.**   The great god of shepherds, flocks, pastures and forests.   He was called a son of Hermes and grandson or great grandson of Kronos (Saturn).   He lived in grottoes, wandering about the mountains and valleys and slumbering during the mid-day heat of summer.   He was also a hunter and led the dances of the nymphs.   As god of the pastoral life he was fond of music and invented the syrinx or shepherd's flute. He exulted in noise and riot and was looked upon as a companion of Cybele and Dionysos.   He is represented in art as a short bearded man with the horns, ears and legs of a goat.   His attributes are a pipe,

crook and the fir tree.  Rams, lambs, milk and honey
were sacrificed to him.  His principal place of worship
was Arcadia, thence it spread to other parts of Greece.
In Rome he was identified with Faunus and Lupercus.
In Egypt the god Pan and a goat were worshipped
at Hermopolis, Lycopolis and Mendes.

**Phœnix.**  This fabulous bird was a common device
in heraldry for those who would convey the impres-
sion of survival.  Queen Elizabeth had the phœnix
stamped upon her medals and coins, frequently with
the motto *Sola phœnix omnis mundi.*  "The only
phœnix in the world."

**Pine Cone.**  A symbol of life among all the Semitic
races.  D'Alviella traces the *cone sacré* to the human
silhouette comparing this also to the *crux ansata*
which shaped the figures of the early nature goddesses
such as Diana of the Ephesians.  The combination
of the sacred cone and the *crux ansata* penetrated to
India where the disk was replaced by an inverted
triangle above the tau.  The symbol in this form is
seen on the footprints of Buddha.

**Playing Cards.**  Besides the enormous diversity of
combination and the mathematical fascination of
cards, it is a curious fact that the four designs are
all symbols of life.  The spade is derived from the leaf
(Bayley identifies leaf with love and life, adding that
it is a scientific fact that a tree lives by its leaves),
the heart is the source of life, the diamond or lozenge

is a symbol of the *yoni* or the feminine principle and the club (*Tréfle* in French) is the trefoil, one of the most ancient symbols of the Trinity or the three-fold aspect of life.

**Pomegranate.** Used by all the Semitic nations as a symbol of fecundity or the passive principle. In the Greek myth pomegranates sprang from the blood of Dionysos, as anemonies from the blood of Adonis and violets from the blood of Attis.

**Poseidon (Neptune).** The god of the waters and the force and flow of life. Among the Greeks the horse, which was likened to a crested sea wave, animated and bridled, was sacred to Poseidon. This may refer to the myth of the contest between Athene and Poseidon for supremacy. Preference was to be given by the assembled gods to the one who gave the most useful present to man. Poseidon struck the earth with his trident and a horse sprang forth. Athene produced the olive and was acclaimed the victor. In art Poseidon is generally represented standing on a dolphin or seated in a chariot formed like a shell and drawn by dolphins or sea horses and holding a trident in his hand.

**Priapus.** The personification of *attraction*. Knight identifies the Greek Bacchus with the First Begotten Love of Orpheus and Hesiod. "In the Orphic Fragments this Deity or First-Begotten Love is said to have been produced together with Ether by Time

(Kronos) or Eternity, and Necessity operating upon inert matter. He is described as eternally begetting, the Father of Night, called in later times the lucid or splendid because he first appeared as splendour; of a double nature as possessing the general power of creation and generation, both active and passive, both male and female. Light is his necessary and primary attribute, co-eternal with himself, and with him brought forth from inert matter by Necessity. Hence the purity and sanctity always attributed to light by the Greeks. . . . He is said to pervade the world with the motion of his wings bringing pure light; and thence to be called the splendid, the ruling Priapus, and self-illumined. . . . The self-created mind of the Eternal Father is said to have spread the heavy bond of love through all things in order that they might endure forever." [1] Geese are sacred to Priapus. He is represented as carrying fruit and either a cornucopia or sickle in his hand. The Italians confounded him with various personifications of the fructifying powers of nature and in Greek legends Priapus is associated with beings who are sensual and licentious. He was the god of gardens and the first fruits of gardens, fields and vineyards were sacrificed to him.

**Psyche** (breath or soul). Psyche is called the "mythical embodiment of the human soul." The

[1] *Worship of Priapus*, R. P. Knight.

myth shows the helplessness, the unreliability, the
tragic suffering of the soul as it passes through the
world of experience.  Quite without consciousness of
anything but beauty and sweetness in life, Psyche
excites the jealous wrath of Aphrodite by the elusive,
intangible, exquisite quality of her beauty.  The myth
resembles the story of Cinderella.  Psyche is beset
by the same forces—the jealous goddess or cruel step-
mother, the twin sisters of pride and envy and Eros
the god of love who, sent by Aphrodite to enchant
her with some monster takes her unto himself and
thus becomes the Prince Charming of the fairy tale.
Eros visits her at night and exacts but one pledge—
that she shall never attempt to see him.  Psyche,
played upon by her envious sisters forgets her promise
and "investigates" love, and love, wounded by her
distrust, flees from her and comes no more.  The rest
of the myth shows the soul paying the price for its
wavering doubts.  Psyche wanders from place to
place searching for her lover.  Finally she comes to
the palace of Aphrodite who recognising and still
hating her makes her a slave.  Eros finding her there
secretly comforts and aids her by his invisible presence.  Her humility and patience win at last even the
goddess of beauty, and Psyche becomes one of the
immortals united forever with Eros.  Psyche and
Eros are frequently represented together in art.
Psyche is often given the wings of a butterfly.

**Ptah.**  The Egyptian Vulcan, the god of fire, Ptah
was also regarded as a form of the sun-god and was
identified with one of the great primeval gods and
called the "father of beginnings and creator of the egg
of the sun and moon."  As creator Ptah was the
embodiment of mind from which all things emerge.
"Ptah was the architect and builder of the material
world."  While Khnemu was fashioning men and
animals Ptah was constructing the heavens and the
earth.  He was represented shaping the egg of the
world on a potter's wheel which he worked with his
foot.  He is usually depicted as a bearded man with
a bald head holding the sceptre of power, the *crux
ansata* and the tat, symbol of stability.

**Ptah-Seker.**  A personification among the Egyptians of the "union of primeval creative power with
a form of the inert powers of darkness or, in other
words Ptah-Seker is a form of Osiris, that is to say,
of the night sun or dead sun-god."  (Budge.)

**Ra.**  The great sun-god of the Egyptians.  He is
generally depicted with the head of a hawk or again
as a hawk.  He has the usual emblems of life and
power, the solar disk and uræus, the *crux ansata* and
sceptre.  He is also identified with the ass, cat, bull,
ram and crocodile.

**Rhea.**  "The name as well as the nature of this
ancient divinity is one of the most difficult points in
ancient mythology."  It is assumed, however, that

like Demeter, Rhea is goddess of the earth. Kronos was said to have devoured all his children by Rhea except Zeus whom she concealed giving Kronos a stone wrapped up as an infant whom the god swallowed. Crete was probably the earliest seat of the worship of Rhea. She was identified with Cybele in Phrygia, was worshipped by the Thracians, under different names she was the great goddess of the Eastern world and was known as the Great Mother, the mother of all the gods. Her priests were the Corybantes who dressed in full armour, with cymbals, horns and drums performed their orgiastic dances on the mountains or in the depths of the forests of Phrygia. Many of the attributes of Rhea were given to her daughter Demeter. The lion was the symbolic animal of the earth-goddess because of all the animals known it was the strongest and most important. In works of art she was rarely depicted standing. She is usually represented seated on a throne, wearing a mural crown from which hangs down a veil. Lions crouch on either side of her throne or sometimes she is shown in a chariot drawn by lions. In Greece the oak tree was sacred to Rhea.

**Sail.** The sail springing into movement under the influence of the wind was an Egyptian symbol of the spirit—*spiritus* meaning breath or wind.

**Salt.** Owing to its incorruptible nature salt was a symbol of immortality. Homer called it divine.

Wisdom is personified holding a salt cellar. "The bestowal of *Sal Sapientiæ*, the Salt of Wisdom, is still a formality in the Latin Church." The victims for sacrifice among the ancient Romans were led to death with salt upon their heads. It was considered the worst possible omen should they shake it off. Hence the superstition about spilling salt. Da Vinci uses this same symbolism in the overturned salt cellar by the side of Judas in his "Last Supper."

**Scarab.** An Egyptian amulet that protected against annihilation.

**Serapeum.** The famous tomb of the Apis bulls at Sakkara. Above stood the great temple of the Serapeum.

**Serapis.** The Egyptians believed that the soul of Apis united itself with Osiris after death and thus became the dual god Asar-Hapi or Osiris-Apis. The Greeks attributed to Asar-Hapi the same qualities of their god Hades and gave it the name of Serapis. Serapis was accepted both by the Greeks and the Egyptians as their principal object of worship and after 250 B.C. it seems to have been looked upon as the male counterpart of Isis. Bronze figures of Apis have a triangular piece of silver in the forehead, a disk and the uræus serpent between the horns, and on the sides of the body the outlined figures of vultures with outstretched wings.

**Set or Typhon.** In the primitive Egyptian religions

Set was not the god of evil but the personification of natural darkness. He was said to be the son of Nut (the sky) and Seb (the earth) and brother of Osiris and Isis. He married his sister Nephthys. In an earlier form he is opposed to Horus the elder. In the second form the combat is between Ra and Set and Set assumes the form of a huge serpent. The third form is Osiris and Set and the fourth is the battle between Horus, son of Osiris and Set. Besides the serpent Apep Set was given the crocodile, pig, turtle, ass and hippopotamus, and animals with reddish brown skins or even red-haired men were supposed to be under his influence and were held in especial aversion. Antelopes and black pigs were sacrificed to him.

**Seven Buddhist Jewels, The.** The golden wheel or disk. Lovely female consorts. Horses. Elephants. Divine guardians of the treasury. Ministers in command of armies. The wonder working pearl. These are the seven gems of a *Chakravarti* or universal monarch. Seven precious jewels also belonged to Brahmanism and are referred to in the Rig-veda.

**Seven Precious Things.** In China and Japan gold, silver, rubies, emeralds, crystal, amber (or coral or the diamond) and agate.

**Seven Wise Ones, The.** These came forth from the eye of Ra and taking the form of seven hawks flew upwards and together with Asten, a form of

Thoth, presided over learning.  Ptah as master architect carried out the designs of Thoth and his Seven
Wise Ones.

**Sistrum.**  An instrument consisting of an oval
metal frame crossed by movable metal bars which
jingle when shaken, and used in the worship of Isis.
"The *sistrum* shows that whatever exists ought to
be shaken and never cease from movement, but should
be aroused and agitated as if it were asleep and its
life quenched.  For they say that by the sistrum they
drove Typhon away; by this they set forth that
destruction binds and halts, but by means of movement generation frees nature."  (Plutarch.)

**Siva.**  The god of destruction or apathy of the
Hindu triad.   Since in Hindu thought destruction
involves restoration, he also represents the principle
of reproduction and his symbols are the phallus
and the bull, typifying the reproductive forces of
nature.

**Stele.**  A term used to denote ancient monoliths
or monuments placed vertically upon which were inscribed historic events or tributes to the memory of
the dead.  *Stelæ* upon which are sculptured the like-
ness of a departed hero or king form some of the most
interesting examples of early Greek and Roman art.
In Egypt the stelæ were originally identical with
the "false doors" of the mastabas and represented
the entrance into the nether world.  They indicated

also the place to which the friends were to turn when
they brought their offerings.

**Suméru or Mt. Méru.** The highest peak of the
Himalayas and supposed to be the centre of the uni-
verse. This is the sacred mountain where dwelt the
Hindu triad Brahma, Vishnu and Siva. Mounts or
Holy Hills were usually three in number. Mt. Méru
had three peaks of gold, silver and iron.

**Surya-mani.** A sun disk surmounted by a trident
is called *surya-mani* or sun jewel. Issuing from the
lotus it represents Adi-Buddha at the creation of
the world.

**Tat, Tet or Zad.** An Egyptian amulet that has
been variously interpreted as symbolising the pole
that measured the Nile, as the tree trunk which enclosed the body of Osiris, or as the back bone of
Osiris, and the setting up of the tat was an important
religious feature in connection with the worship of
the god. The tat pole has been called an Egyptian
type of the "pole or pillar that sustained the universe."
The tat like the Buckle amulet of Isis had to be dipped
in water in which *ankham* flowers had lain and was
hung around the mummy's neck for its protection.
The word denotes stability, firmness, preservation.

**Thet or Buckle amulet of Isis.** This represents a
girdle made of carnelian, red jasper or red glass and is
also called the "carnelian girdle tie of Isis." It
brought to the deceased the protection of Isis giving

him access, moreover, to every place in the world of shades.

**Thoth, Thot, Thaut or Tehuti.** The Egyptian god of learning, the scribe, the "pathfinder and awakener of sleeping minds." He is a moon-god and his symbol the ibis. He is frequently depicted with the head of an ibis. The baboon was also sacred to Thoth.

**Thrones.** Three thrones surmounted by royal caps symbolised the great Babylonian triad Anu, Enlil and Ea. Thrones who support the seat of the Most High belong to the nine-fold celestial hierarchy of the early Christians. These were symbolised as fiery wheels surrounded by wings and the wings filled with eyes.

**Thyrsus.** A staff entwined with ivy or vine branches or sometimes with a knot of ribbon and surmounted by a pine cone, the symbol of life. Bacchus and his followers carry the thyrsus. It was also used in their religious ceremonies by the Egyptians, Phœnicians, Greeks and Jews.

**Torii.** The temple gateway in Japan consisting of two upright and two horizontal beams of bronze, copper or stone, symbolising peace and rest or the Gateway of Life. It is said in Japan that the sun-goddess frequently descends to earth in the form of the "heavenly phœnix" making the *torii* her perch.

**Trilobe or Trefoil.** A form much used in mullions and arcades of the Gothic architecture and derived from the cloverleaf or the outer rim of three circles, one above two, both of which were ancient symbols of the Trinity.

**"Trimurti."**  The Hindu triad, Brahma the Creator, Vishnu the Preserver and Siva the Destroyer or Apathy.

**Triquetra.**  A mystical three-pointed ornament derived from three elongated circles without beginning or end and forming a symbolical *motif* in architectural decoration.

**Tri-ratna.**  The "three precious jewels," Buddha, Dharma and Sangha whose symbols are the trisula, the syllable a.u.m. and the triangle.

**Umbrella or Parasol.**  An emblem of royalty universally adopted by Eastern nations and carried over the head of a king in times of peace and sometimes in war.  Like the halo it is derived from the solar wheel and is placed over the head of Buddha as a symbol of power.

**Unicorn's Horn.**  The belief that the unicorn typified purity and virtue led to the further belief that the horn of the animal had the power of revealing treasons and was an antidote against poisons.  In the Middle Ages the smallest piece of anything that purported to be this rare horn commanded a price ten times more than its weight in gold.  The unicorn's horn now in the Musée Cluny, Paris (in reality a narwhal's tusk) was presented to Charlemagne by the Sultan Haroun-al-Raschid in 807, deposited by

URÆUS SERPENT.  XXVI DYNASTY
(Metropolitan Museum of Art.)

SNAKE AND VULTURE.  XXVI–XXX DYNASTY
(Metropolitan Museum of Art.)

BOWL WITH DECORATIONS OF FISHES, CYPRIOTE. LATE BRONZE
AGE (1500–2000 B.C.)
(Metropolitan Museum of Art.)

CANOPIC JARS OF SENESTISI. XII DYNASTY
(Metropolitan Museum of Art.)

the emperor in the imperial treasury at Aix-la-Chapelle, and afterwards placed by his grandson Charles the Bald in the treasury of the abbey church of St. Denis where it was jealously guarded for 950 years as a potent means of protecting the French kings against poisoning. It bears the scars of various notches.

**Uræus Serpent.** The uræus was an Egyptian symbol of royalty and power and worn on the king's crown was supposed to spit venom on the king's enemies.

**Ûrnâ.** The shining spot in Buddha's forehead, the sign of spiritual consciousness, symbol of the "eye divine" and later developed as the third eye of Siva.

**Uzat.** The mystic eye. An Egyptian amulet which, when worn by a cord around the neck, was a protection against malice, envy, evil. The Uzat or Eye of Horus was also a charm against the evil eye, which was as greatly feared in Egypt as in Italy. [See Eye.]

**Venus.** [See Aphrodite.]

**Vishnu.** His Three Strides are his position at dawn, at noon and in the evening. The garuda bird half-giant, half-eagle was his vehicle and his symbol, the discus, is identified with the Wheel of the Law.

**Vulcan.** [See Hephæstos.]

**Willow Branch.** With it Kwan-yin the Chinese goddess of mercy sprinkles about her the divine nectar of life.   The willow branch is sometimes depicted in a vase.

**Wood.**   Swedenborg makes wood a symbol of "celestial goodness in its lowest corporeal plane."

**Zen.**   The absolute is immanent in every man's heart.   There is no use seeking Buddha outside your own nature—no Buddha but your own thoughts. Zen means "for a man to behold his own fundamental nature."   Buddha is thought.

**Zeus (Jupiter).**   In Greek art Zeus is always represented as a bearded man of noble and majestic mien. His attributes are the eagle, the sceptre and the thunderbolt.   The thunderbolt in his hand typifies that he is the origin, beginning, middle and end of all things.   He is heaven, earth, fire, water, day and night. His eyes are the sun and moon.   He is space and eternity, the essence and life of all beings.   He is sometimes represented in sitting posture in allusion to his immutable essence, the upper part of his body uncovered, typifying the upper regions of the universe, and covered from the waist down because in terrestrial things he is more secret and concealed.   He holds the sceptre in the left hand because the heart is on the left side and the heart is the seat of understanding.

# INDEX

---

[1] Gibbon relates that among the early Romans "The communion of the marriage-life was denoted by the necessary elements of fire and water." He adds in a footnote that this acceptance of fire and water was considered as the essence of marriage. Gibbon's *Decline and Fall of Rome.* Vol. VII, pp. 316–317.